Revolutionary Romances?

Edited by
Staatliche Kunstsammlungen Dresden
Mathias Wagner | Hilke Wagner
and
Kerstin Schankweiler | Kathleen Reinhardt

Global Art Histories
in the GDR

Raúl Martínez, El Che y Camilo, 1968, film poster, color screen print, 81.3 × 38.2 cm, Kupferstich-Kabinett, Staatliche Kunstsammlungen Dresden, inv. no. A 2020–11

Jürgen Nagel, Ho Chi Minh high school, Berlin-Friedrichshagen, 1979, silver gelatine paper, 20.5 × 29.5 cm, Kupferstich-Kabinett, Staatliche Kunstsammlungen Dresden, inv. no. D 1985–98
The slogan on the banner runs: "Our goal for the 30th anniversary [of the GDR]: 100,000 105,000 [East German] marks of solidarity!"

Signature campaign in protest against the assassination of Congolese prime minister Patrice Lumumba, Dresden, January 1961. photo: Erich Höhne & Erich Pohl

Hilke Wagner

Revolutionary Romances?
Global Art Histories in the GDR

For some years now, thinking the history of art (as) in global (connected) terms and overcoming the idea of an art canon that is singular, Western and linear has become common international practice and is also the cause of numerous research and exhibition projects in Germany. However, art from the GDR has so far been largely disregarded—considered to be a special case—and predominantly characterized as "provincial", "self-referential", and "isolated". Therefore, a broad transcultural perspective on art in the GDR is both highly relevant and overdue in order to refute predominant perceptions and fundamentally rethink its history in terms of an "art history of contact".[1]

The Albertinum has already carried out several projects along these lines in recent years. The exhibition *The Medea Insurrection. Radical Women Artists Behind the Iron Curtain* (2018/2019) presented subversive female artists from the GDR along with female artists from the Eastern Bloc.[2] The exhibition *1 Million Roses for Angela Davis* (2020/2021) shed light on connections with representatives of the "other America" and was the first to examine the ambiguous topic of the solidarity propagated in the light of the GDR's supposed decolonial and anti-racist attitude.[3]

Our multiyear research and exhibition project *Revolutionary Romances? Global Art Histories in the GDR* puts the focus on the complex relations between the GDR and the "Global South". The basis for this urgent historical reappraisal of art and culture is provided by the rich collections of the Dresden State Art Collection (SKD)—in particular the Albertinum, the Kupferstich-Kabinett (Museum of Prints, Drawings and Photographs) and the Kunstfonds (Art Fund)—, which more than anything mirror the GDR's links with socialist and socialist-oriented countries in Africa, Asia, and Latin America. Our collections also reflect the international exhibition and collection history of the GDR and attest to its ambitions in the realm of foreign policy—with works covering everything from the foundation up to the collapse of the Eastern Bloc. The starting point of this research project is the analysis of the multilayered relational structure and the mutual forms of influence that exist in the enterprise of a socialist internationalism. Its first results were presented during a prolog exhibition in 2020[4], while two international conventions held that same year at the Albertinum lead to a further widening of the field of study to incorporate important aspects, including from the perspective of former "brother countries" of the GDR.[5]

The regularly rekindled "Bilderstreit" (picture controversy) between Eastern and Western Germany, is clear proof of the degree to which East-West German art history still operates in a self-referential manner. Its vigorous reignition during the fall of 2017 revealed a substantial need for further debate, regarding not only the museological handling of art from the GDR but also its scientific reappraisal and integration into a broader historiography of art. As it turned out, this "Bilderstreit" was not only a proxy debate which gave voice to

1   Christian Kravagna: Transmoderne – Eine Kunstgeschichte des Kontakts, Berlin 2017.
2   The Medea Insurrection. Radical Women Artists Behind the Iron Curtain, Kunsthalle im Lipsiusbau, Dresden, 8.12.2018–31.3.2019.
3   1 Million Roses for Angela Davis, Kunsthalle im Lipsiusbau, Dresden, 10.10.2020–30.5.2021.
4   Revolutionary Romances. Transcultural Art Histories in the GDR | Prolog, Albertinum, Dresden, 13.4.–17.7.2022 (extended 4.9.2022).
5   The Global GDR. A Transcultural History of Art (1949–1990), jointly organized by TU Dresden and the Albertinum of the Dresden State Art Collections, supported by Fritz Thyssen Stiftung, Albertinum, Dresden, 9.–11.6.2022. Recording of the contributions: https://voices.skd.museum/en/voices-mag/the-global-gdr-a-transcultural-history-of-art-1949-1990/ (accessed on: 11.10.2023); Into the Cold. Alternative Artistic Trajectories into (Post-) Communist Europe, supported by the Terra Foundation for American Art and the Goethe Institute, Albertinum, Dresden, 13.10.2022. Recording of the contributions: https://voices.skd.museum/en/voices-mag/revolutionary-romances-into-the-cold-alternative-trajectories-into-post-communist-europe/ (accessed on: 11.10.2023).

unprocessed traumas and frustration stemming from a "reunification" process that was felt
highly problematic from an Eastern German perspective. It was, in essence, also a controversy
about concepts of art which all too often revealed certain expectations of respect for an
established and seemingly sacrosanct canon. Starting from here can offer an opportunity—
for introducing the concept of a global history of art to a larger audience and necessary
critical reflections, also in terms of a process of institutional decolonization which resolutely
leverages established local narratives to expose existing links to the little-known global
dimension. The Albertinum, which was in itself part of the supposed "Revolutionary
Romances", in its functions as an exhibition space and collection, offers the opportunity to
contemplate this art history of entanglements in the mirror of its own past. It can contrast
the current concepts with its own history—which differs from the histories of museums in
Western Germany—and add important aspects to a globally mediated history of art.

During the Cold War era, the Dresden State Art Collections frequently served as a
diplomatic tool. From a present-day perspective, the absence of any scope for actual anti-
imperialistic thought and action is conspicuous. The twin concepts of "international
friendship" and "solidarity", which played a central role in the GDR's ideological orientation
and presented—as regularly propagated ideals—a foundation for not least of all politically
and economically motivated alliances in the Global South, are nowadays—in the face of
growing disintegration—more relevant than ever. It is, however, essential that they be
conceived in all their ambiguity as instruments of the foreign and domestic politics of a
dictatorial system. While the GDR pursued an active cultural diplomacy, it isolated foreign
contract workers within its own "actually existing socialism". Working conditions were
difficult, any "fraternization" between contract workers and GDR citizens was everything
but welcome, and everyday racism was very common. Ambiguities such as these are
analyzed by artists such as Sung Tieu, who is herself a member of the second generation of
the Vietnamese community in Eastern Germany and who spent part of her childhood
in Freital near Dresden (p. 110/111). Sung Tieu and the other artists presented in the exhibition
(Georges Adéagbo, Sven Johne, Hamlet Lavastida, Dana Lorenz, Sonya Schönberger,
Wenke Seemann, and Arlette Quỳnh-Anh Trần) enter into a dialogue with the historic
positions and firmly root the exhibition in the present—a crucial step in a location like
Dresden, where many former contract workers still live and where postsocialism meets postcolonialism on a daily basis.

First and foremost, I would like to thank our former curator Kathleen Reinhardt, who has
been working on the idea for this exhibition project since 2017. Equally, I would like to
thank our conservator Mathias Wagner, who had participated in the planning as a co-curator
before taking over from Kathleen Reinhardt after her departure and adopting the project
as his own in a wonderful manner. He had the active support of our trainee Pauline Hohn
and our assistant curator Martin Buhlig. And we all thank our cooperation partners,
the Kunstfonds and the Kupferstich-Kabinett, as well as the archive of the Hochschule für
Bildende Künste Dresden (Dresden Academy of Fine Arts) for supporting our research
into the lives of foreign students.

Sophie Hundbiss and Laurentius Alvin designed a comprehensive education and mediation
program for the exhibition, with numerous external partners and the active involvement
of various communities. We thank them and the entire Department of Education and
Communication from the heart. That program was made possible through the support of
the Bundeszentrale für politische Bildung (Federal Agency for Civic Education). We would
like to thank Prof. Dr. Kerstin Schankweiler (TU Dresden/Dresden University of Technology)
and her colleagues for an inspiring cooperation, notably in the course of conventions and
conferences. Their project *Art in Networks—The GDR and its Global Relations* was incorporated
into the exhibition. This important project could not have been realized without the
support of the Kulturstiftung des Bundes (German Federal Cultural Foundation)—therefore,

8

thank you very much! Moreover, we thank the Peter und Irene Ludwig Stiftung (Peter and Irene Ludwig Foundation) for their support, especially in terms of content and loans.

Last but not least, we express our gratitude to the participating artists. While our exhibition approaches the aforementioned topics from "within" an institutional inventory, they are simultaneously examined from without by Doreen Mende, head of the Department of Research at the SKD. In 2024, three interventions of artists and curators from the Global South are performed in the permanent exhibition of the Albertinum as part of her long-term research project *Decolonizing Socialism: Entangled Internationalism*.[6] These are first steps that contribute to an already ongoing institutional rethinking of the Albertinum that also concerns the presentation of its collection which must make the results of this research project visible.

6   See Doreen Mende's contribution in this volume, p. 159–162.

Umberto Peña Garriga, Dictatorships in America, n. d., woodcut, 100 × 280 cm, Kupferstich-Kabinett, Staatliche Kunstsammlungen Dresden, inv. no. A 1963–22

Pedro Pablo Oliva, Explosion, 1969, lithograph in four colors, 53.8 × 37.5 cm, Kupferstich-Kabinett, Staatliche Kunstsammlungen Dresden, inv. no. B 1970–281

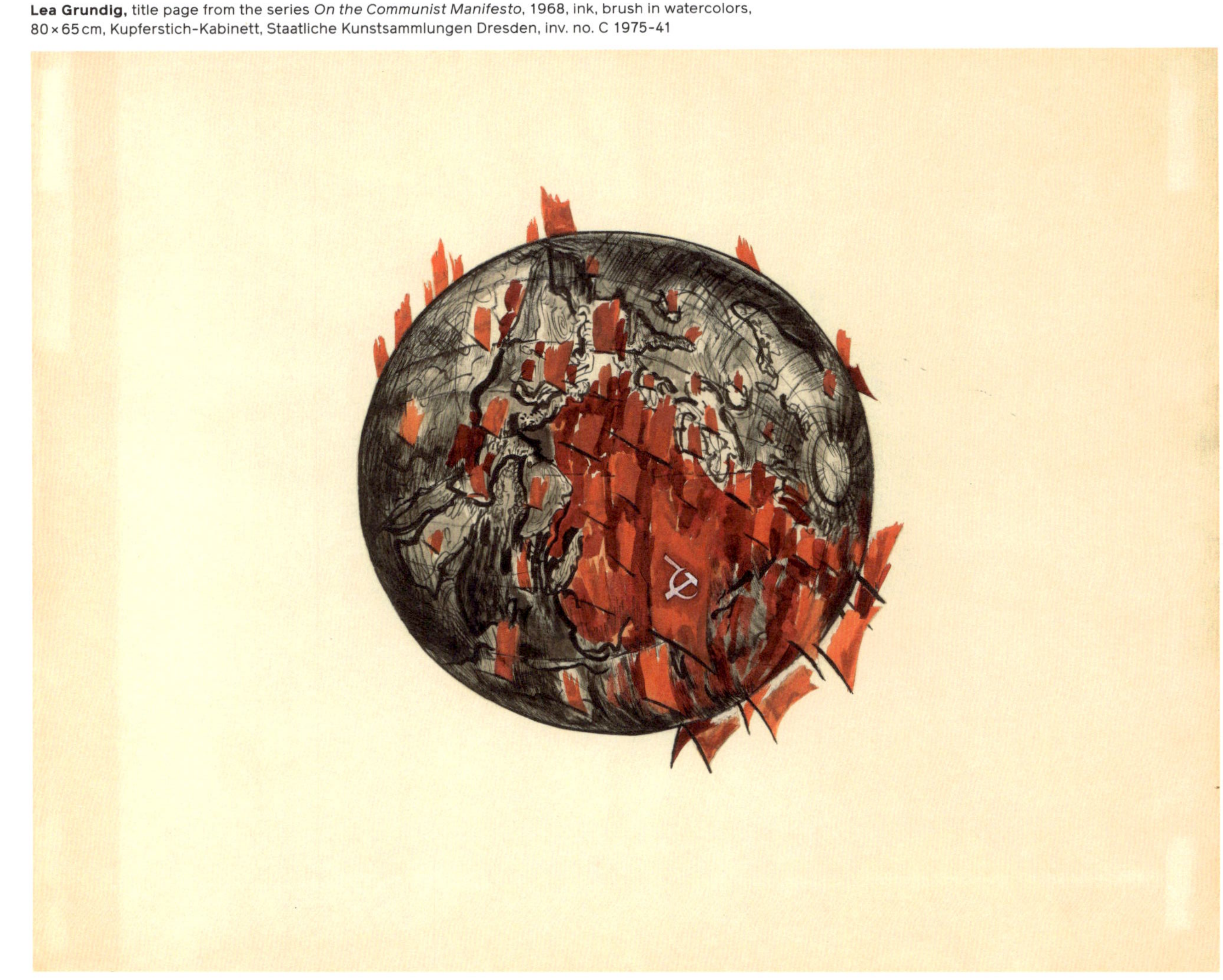

Lea Grundig, title page from the series *On the Communist Manifesto*, 1968, ink, brush in watercolors, 80 × 65 cm, Kupferstich-Kabinett, Staatliche Kunstsammlungen Dresden, inv. no. C 1975–41

Borders often mark the accentuation of ideological concepts between "insiders" and "outsiders" and thus determine belonging or no belonging. The inside and outside are negotiated in confrontation with the border and determine the conditions under which a member of a society has access. Differences in language as well as in social and political structures become evident. Within a society, such ideological borders strengthen cultural, moral, religious, and social rules and hence determine their mechanism for creating identity. Fundamental questions can be derived from this, for example, how borders affect neighboring regions, what practices of drawing borders are employed, and which dynamics result within the bordered regions. This also raises questions of the extent to which innovative energy and creativity grow out of the experience of the border or how much cross-border (transcultural) exchange takes place and what forms the transfer takes (appropriation, rejection, reinterpretation, translation, etc.), and which interactions and dissolutions of borders occur. Borders are complex constructions that establish identity and depend substantially on their spatial and temporal structure, and are therefore transient. Borders that at a certain time seemed immovable can seem almost obsolete today. What effects does it have on constructions of identity when borders are removed—for example, for the people in eastern and western Germany after reunification?

More than thirty years after the separation of Germany was overcome, it is time, especially in the eastern states, to enter a phase of conciliatory, empathetic, and social exchange. Empathy means developing the ability to adopt and accept other perspectives of perception and experience. For example, if one takes stock with an eye to assessment the art history of the two Germanys and to the large exhibitions of recent years that presented art from four decades of the GDR, one hears warning voices: "A canon is currently becoming established that has nothing to do with the perspectives of those who experienced the era." (Matthias Flügge)

Taking this as an occasion, with the *Kontrapunkte* project (counterpoints) of the past two years, the Staatliche Kunstsammlungen Dresden (SKD; Dresden State Art Collections) has dedicated itself to an area in the history of art and culture that is particularly connected to the history of the institution and the place, where one would perhaps least expect global networking: the era of the GDR. A chapter of German history that for many people in our country—not just older East Germans—triggers emotional reactions and embraces multi-layered social, political, and cultural aspects—indeed, entire life plans. The SKD is building on long-standing, fundamental research that has already flowed into many projects and publications. To name just a few examples: *Bildatlas. Kunst der DDR / Picture Atlas. Art from the GDR* (2009–12), the publication *Sozialistisch sammeln / Collecting Socialistically* (2014), and numerous small and large exhibitions at various SKD museums, such as *Geniale Dilletanten. Subkultur der 1980er Jahre in West- und Ostdeutschland / Brilliant Dilletantes. Subculture in West and East Germany in the 1980s* (2017), *Ostdeutsche Malerei und Skulptur 1949–1990 / East German Painting and Sculpture 1949–1990* (2018–19), *Medea muckt auf. Radikale Künstlerinnen hinter dem Eisernen Vorhang / The Medea Insurrection. Radical Women Artists Behind the Iron Curtain* (2018–19), *1 Million Rosen für Angela Davis / 1 Million Roses for Angela Davis* (2020–21), and *Deutsches Design 1949–1989. Zwei Länder—eine Geschichte / German Design 1949–1989. Two Countries—one History* (2021–22).

Begun with the goal of countering codifications from multiple perspectives and thus shaking them up, the projects that have led to this special exhibition and publication leave room for the complexity of diverse microhistories or even individual "autobiographical truths." With *Revolutionary Romances?* the SKD are taking part in a broad societal discourse and question a one-dimensional view or history with transdisciplinary and transcultural programs, exhibitions, and discursive formats. This succeeds by allowing many different voices to speak, by exposing both grievances and stories of success, and recognizing shared historical facts to drive a "new relational ethics" (Bénédicte Savoy).

In addition, deductive and inductive approaches were combined to get close to a "truth" that lies in complexity, diversity, and contradictoriness. The points of references lie both inside and outside of the SKD. Inside, the collections are studied by scholars and curators of the SKD with regard to their historical entanglements with processes from the GDR era. The current exhibition presents, among other things, extensive research results and a number of microhistories of these transcultural relationships of the GDR using examples from our collections.

Even thirty years after the fall of the Berlin Wall, the eye repeatedly gets caught up in that "no man's land" between the autumn of 1989 and the autumn of 1990. And the question floating over everything then, still unanswered today, as asked anew with greater urgency: What impulses form the eastern part of Germany could then and can still bear fruit for the global process? Or to put it another way: The question whether something developed in the greenhouse atmosphere of the East that would enrich the overall development—also in connection with Eastern European countries—has not yet been answered fully despite the numerous activities of the past thirty years.

These and many more questions that revolve around our relationship to the GDR have resulted in a program series that from the institution outward integrates both historical eyewitnesses and generations born later who demand answers.

In laboratories spanning multiple collections, the employees of the SKD have worked with local and international experts from art, culture, and politics as well as with interested parties among the city's residents have reflected on and discussed a variety of themes. For example, with impressive openness, the youth committee of SKD's *FUTUR III* and former manufacturers from Meissen have joined in a dialogue. No less open, designers met at the *Round Table* and shared their experiences. All of the events were broadcast live and then archived on *voices*, the digital platform of the SKD, thus making them available to the public.

With the opening of the exhibition *Revolutionary Romances?* and the accompanying publication, a forward-looking project of two years of intense research, fruitful exchange, and innovative education work has reached a high point—perhaps just a first high point, because this occasion can be described at the same time as a beginning. Additional labs will form, continuing the research and developing new exhibition concepts. We remain open!

In the name of all of us from the Staatliche Kunstsammlungen Dresden who have been involved in this project, I sincerely thank the German Federal Cultural Foundation and the Peter and Irene Ludwig Foundation whose generous support made the exhibition and publication possible. I thank the Federal Center for Political Education for supporting selected education and outreach projects as part of the exhibition and on our digital platform *voices*.

Marion Ackermann
Director General

Ines Johnson-Spain's life story begins with a 'revolutionary romance.' Her parents met in East Berlin in the 1960s—she was a married GDR citizen, he a guest student from Togo. Johnson-Spain is the product of their love story. She was adopted by her mother's husband and grew up in the GDR as a Black child of *white* parents. The family never mentioned the biological father and instead told the child that skin color is distributed at random. Consequently, Johnson's childhood was marked by embarrassing silences within her family, malicious glee from neighbors, and racist hostility from state institutions. This 'romance', as described in Johnson-Spain's autobiographical film *Becoming Black* (2019), is a poignant representation of the historical political situation explored in the exhibition *Revolutionary Romances? Global Art Histories in the GDR* at the Albertinum, a part of the Staatliche Kunstsammlungen Dresden (SKD; Dresden State Art Collections).

Revolutionary Romances? provides an artistic language for a hitherto little-explored and discussed historical experience in the GDR. Based on the comprehensive holdings of the Staatliche Kunstsammlungen Dresden, the exhibition assembles works of art from the phase of the GDR's propagandized friendly-revolutionary relationship with countries of the Global South. In terms of cultural politics, these global relationships were pursued with the grand gesture of a Socialist peace project. The utopian horizon was a globally networked society without inequalities. These works from the SKD collection are complemented by selected national loans, and they vividly convey the hopes for a new, transnational community after the Second World War as well as Euro-centric superiority fantasies. They reveal how colonial power relations and racist attributions to the supposed brothers and sisters were ideologically perpetuated in the GDR, partly through exoticizing, paternalistic or pejorative ideas about the lives of people in the alleged partner countries. Some very different, sometimes also violent memories are juxtaposed in the diversity of the exhibited art from Cuba, Chile, Vietnam, India, Iraq, Libya, Mozambique, Burma (Myanmar), and the GDR, among other places. Historical works are interrogated by contemporary creations, such as those of Sung Tieu and Wenke Seemann. Here, it is the generation of the daughters who, through their own artistic production, force into the open what had been left unspoken of their parents' experience as migrants in the GDR.

The exhibition stimulates an exchange about the contradictions of the Socialist progress project, which unavoidably affected both individual and state relationships. In the context of the ongoing virulent debate about the critical examination of colonialism and its consequences in East and West Germany, it is important to draw public attention to this subject. *Revolutionary Romances?,* and the accompanying project *Kontrapunkte* (counterpoints), can build on existing scholarly and artistic debates, tie them together, and initiate a discussion with the Dresden audience. The German Federal Cultural Foundation wishes the Dresden State Art Collections, their general director, Marion Ackermann, the director of the Albertinum Hilke Wagner, the exhibition curator Mathias Wagner and the entire team every success and many exciting conversations with visitors.

Katarzyna Wielga-Skolimowska
Executive Board / Artistic Director

Kirsten Haß
Executive Board / Administrative Director

It is a fundamental objective of the Peter and Irene Ludwig Foundation to contribute to a worldwide dialogue and an inspiring engagement with art through its collection and funding activities. To this end, the foundation cooperates internationally with a wide-ranging network of publicly funded museums. Everyone should experience outstanding works of art and exhibitions, engage with them, and take away new impressions, perspectives, and insights. We consider ourselves fortunate to have knowledgeable curators who develop new scholarly perspectives. The exhibition *Revolutionary Romances? Global Art Histories in the GDR* is an excellent example of how this can be achieved. It uses works of art from the GDR times to highlight an aspect of art history as well as the Ludwig Collection that has received little attention to date.

In the second half of the twentieth century, Irene and Peter Ludwig built up one of the most important and comprehensive art collections of the time, including substantial bodies of work by artists from the GDR. When asked about the overwhelming panorama of cultures, nationalities and epochs in their collection, the couple often used the term "Weltkunst" (world art).

The Ludwigs attached very real questions and hopes to this intriguing term, which seems almost a little rose-tinted if one considers current debates on globalization. They saw great potential in the holistic view of different cultures and their artistic testimonies as contemporary documents. And they were convinced that by discovering similarities on the one hand and specific characteristics and differences on the other, they would promote mutual understanding and dialogue—across the boundaries of cultures, political systems and nations. This aspiration was not merely rhetorical: Irene and Peter Ludwig pursued it purposefully with every single work of art they acquired and with every decision as to which institution they would donate it to.

Thus, in 1977 the Ludwigs presented a long-term loan of works "from the West"—including pieces by Pablo Picasso, Jean Tinguely, and Horst Antes, as well as Roy Lichtenstein, Jasper Johns, and Robert Rauschenberg—to the National Gallery in East Berlin. In return, on January 13, 1979, an exhibition opened in Aachen—at the westernmost edge of the Federal Republic of Germany—featuring works by some of the most renowned, state-approved artists of the GDR, including Bernhard Heisig, Wolfgang Mattheuer, Willi Sitte, and Werner Tübke. The exhibition *Kunst heute in der Deutschen Demokratischen Republik* showed new acquisitions by the collectors. It should not be glossed over at this point that the works by the then dissident A. R. Penck, which had initially also been selected, were ultimately not put on display and that the exhibition was the subject of a heated debate.

We could cite countless other examples to shed light on the way the Ludwigs operated between the most diverse conceptions, and to illustrate their thinking in both directions. However controversial their endeavors may have been at one time or another, they are clearly guided by a desire for discovery and the idea of mediation, both of which are formative for the Ludwigs' collection and funding activities. For us as a foundation today, open-mindedness, a love of art and curiosity towards new interrelationships are important guiding principles. We are therefore delighted to lend the project *Revolutionary Romances?* our support.

Carla Cugini
Chief Executive Officer

Alfredo González Rostgaard, Untitled (Christ as Guerilla Fighter), 1969, OSPAAAL poster, offset print, 53×33cm. Kupferstich-Kabinett, Staatliche Kunstsammlungen Dresden, inv. no. A 2021-43

Heinz Lohmar, Adenike, 1960, oil on hardboard, 114 × 88 cm, Albertinum, Staatliche Kunstsammlungen Dresden, inv. no. 70/17

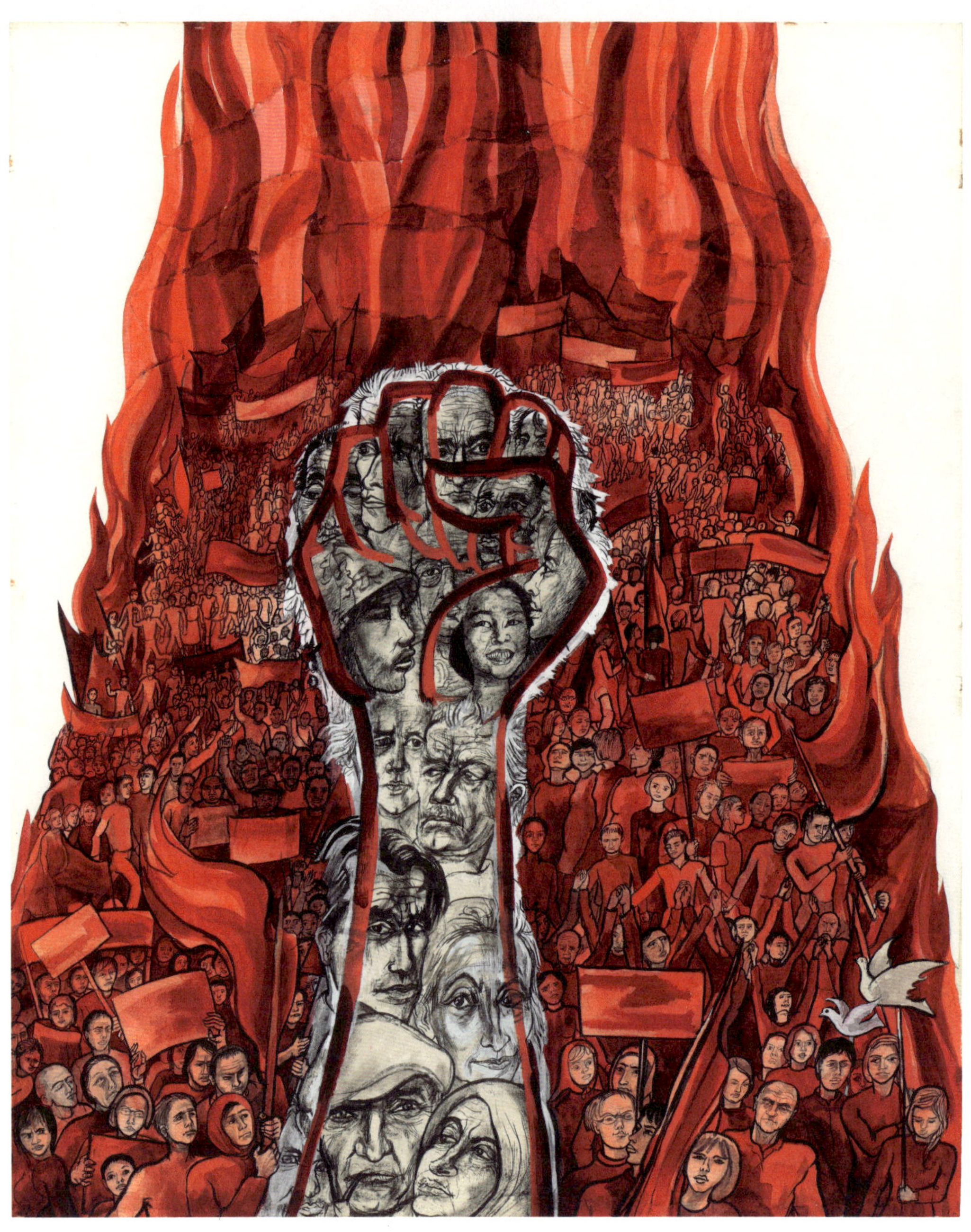

Lea Grundig, *Proletarians of All Countries*, sheet 11 from the series *On the Communist Manifesto*, 1968, ink, watercolor, 85.2 × 70.2 cm, Kupferstich-Kabinett, Staatliche Kunstsammlungen Dresden, inv. no. C 1975-50

Malangatana Valente Ngwenya, Brotamos por todos es lados por mais que nos destruam (We sprout everywhere, no matter how much they destroy us), before 1974, drawing, 69 × 50 cm, GRASSI Museum für Völkerkunde zu Leipzig, inv. no. MAf 35332

Elena Serrano, Day Of The Heroic Guerrilla October 8, OSPAAAL poster, offset print, 50 × 33 cm, Kupferstich-Kabinett, Staatliche Kunstsammlungen Dresden, inv. no. A 2021-50

Kathleen Reinhardt, Kerstin Schankweiler, Mathias Wagner

Internationalism in the GDR— Art and Visual Culture between Ideals and Contradictions

A poster with the likeness of Che Guevara, a hero of the Cuban Revolution. A portfolio with woodcuts and aphorisms by the Ethiopian artist Martha Ketsela, printed in the graphic arts workshops of the Hochschule für Bildende Künste (Dresden Academy of Fine Arts, p. 90/91). A series of photographs documenting the work lives of Vietnamese contract workers at the VEB Herrenmode (men's fashion state-owned company) in Dresden (p. 104/105). An exhibition with paintings and batik by Sumana Dissanayake of Sri Lanka at the Museum für Völkerkunde (Museum of Ethnology) in Dresden. The traces of socialist visual culture and art from the years 1949 to 1990 in the museums of the Staatliche Kunstsammlungen Dresden (SKD; Dresden State Art Collections) point far beyond the German Democratic Republic (GDR) and the Eastern Bloc. They are testimony to an internationalism that was often staged in an almost dreamy way. They are filled with the realities of life in real socialism when we learn that the Che Guevara poster was part of a larger group of works that a curator at the Dresdner Kupferstich-Kabinett (Museum of Prints, Drawings and Photographs) brought back from an official trip to Cuba that also served as an opportunity to get permission to marry a Cuban woman who was living in the GDR.[1] Or that East German artists had better odds of participating in one of the GDR's art exhibitions at the Albertinum in Dresden if they submitted a popular motif of "anti-imperialist solidarity." Or the extent to which the living conditions of the contract workers portrayed were determined by exclusion, restrictive rules, and daily racism.[2]

The exhibition *Revolutionary Romances? Global Art Histories in the GDR* looks at the GDR's friendly, revolutionary relationships with socialist countries and movements in Asia, Africa, and Latin America and hence a chapter of art in the GDR that has hardly been studied at all. The progressive, idealist thesis in the title is a reminder of the hope for a socialist-oriented internationalism at the time. At the same time, the question mark alludes, especially in retrospect, to the obvious ambivalences and contradictions of that utopia.

The Politics of Socialist Internationalism

As geopolitically and ideologically motivated concepts, "international solidarity" and "international friendship" shaped East German foreign policy and flanked a number of transcultural contacts and encounters. They included, for example, international exhibition cooperations, travel by artists, trips for foreign students to study at art schools in the GDR, and the exchange of works of art as a diplomatic gesture. These cultural activities spanned almost the entire globe, but the GDR sought above all to be close to states and movements

1   Olaf Simon: "Somos ejemplo del mundo". Zur Erwerbungsgeschichte kubanischer Kunst am Dresdner Kupferstich-Kabinett, in: Dresdener Kunstblätter 64 (2020), no. 3, p. 5–11, here p. 8–9.
2   On the discrepancy between an official antiracist narrative of the society and the daily lives of "East Germans of color," see Patrice G. Poutrus, Katharina Warda: Ostdeutsche of Color. Schwarze Geschichte(n) der DDR und Erfahrungen nach der deutschen Einheit, in: Aus Politik und Zeitgeschichte, March 18, 2022: https://www.bpb.de/shop/zeitschriften/apuz/schwarz-und-deutsch-2022/506171/ostdeutsche-of-color/ (accessed on: 11.10.2023); Ankunft, Alltag, Ausreise. Migration und Interkulturalität in der DDR-Gesellschaft, ed. Christian T. Müller, Patrice G. Poutrus, Köln 2005; Peggy Piesche: Black and German? East German Adolescents before 1989: A Retrospective View of a "Non-Existent Issue" in the GDR, in: The Cultural After-Life of East Germany: New Transnational Perspectives, ed. Leslie A. Adelson, Washington 2002, p. 37–59.

MALEREI UND BATIK
Sumana Dissanayake – Sri Lanka

already following the socialist model (or at least tending in the direction of socialism), which were viewed as "natural allies." This internationalism—often dramatized with great pathos in the media—was not without contradictions.[3] It competed with the concept of the nation-state and the boundaries of realpolitik but it was of central importance to the recognition by international law that the GDR hoped to receive. The network of "socialist fraternal countries" for which it was striving can be understood as an anti-capitalist alternative to the Western globalization of the postwar era. The GDR implemented this in the form of an "internationalism as model of bureaucratized diplomacy,"[4] as Chelsea Haines and Gemma Sharpe describe it. Despite the many deficits that resulted from it, internationalism was an ideal that persuaded many people in the socialist world and that they were able to fill with life—in their art as well.

Between the imagined and propagated "international socialist community," on the one hand, which was to be manifested exemplarily in artistic work as well, and the real, more practical forms of transcultural exchange, on the other, an area of tension emerged in which international liaisons in art can be studied in greater detail. On the one hand, this can shed light on unknown freedoms beyond Eurocentric narratives; on the other hand, it reveals a system of unfreedoms, restrictions on contacts, constraints, and discriminations that extends into the present. For example, the maxim of socialist coexistence on equal footing does not protect against paternalism, exoticism, stereotypes, and racism. Following on the standard work edited by Quinn Slobodian, *Comrades of Color. East Germany in the Cold War World,*[5] the continuities of racism in the visual worlds of socialism can be worked out using the example of art. They in turn can be connected to current debates over the neocolonial conduct of the West and over racist socialization in Germany without shifting the problem of racism in Germany to the GDR and East Germany, downplaying its causes, and thus once again continuing to confirm West Germany's narrative as victor. It is rather about exposing contradictions and rifts in the large leftist counterproject of the twentieth century that propagated secularism, universalism, and egalitarianism but did not honor those values in a form tied to the state.

Looking at the GDR's international relationships brings to light many other voids, hierarchies, and exclusions. It takes on an importance on the subject of transnational contacts by the fact that is difficult to resolve from the fact that as a rule it was directed, restricted, and controlled by the state and by institutions and therefore those in conflict with the state

3   See also Jérome Bazin, Pascal Dubourg Glatigny, Piotr Piotrowski: Introduction. Geography of Internationalism, in: Art beyond Borders. Artistic Exchange in Communist Europe (1945–1989), eds. Jérôme Bazin, Pascal Dubourg Glatigny, Piotr Piotrowski, Budapest, New York 2016, p. 1–28.

4   Chelsea Haines, Gemma Sharpe: Art, Institutions, and Internationalism, 1945–73, in: ARTMargins 8 (2019), no. 2, p. 3–14.

5   Quinn Slobodian, ed., Comrades of Color. East Germany in the Cold War, New York 2015.

Solidarity banner of the Printing and Paper Workers' Union, Grimma Regional Executive Committee, 1975, photo: Gerhard Weber

were excluded from the outset. Does focusing on international connections accordingly once again disadvantage artists who did not conform and were marginalized in the GDR?

Recent history of the art of the GDR that divides into an official camp and a dissident one fails to register the complex realities of the lives of artists. Rarely can they be assigned exclusively to one of these poles. Rather, they are distinguished by the changing strategies between conformity and self-will with which they tried to get by as artists in the repressive power structures of the dictatorship. The traces of internationalism in formerly socialist countries must, moreover, be understood in their efforts not only to illustrate the socialist world but also to influence the project of socialism in critical and constructive ways. The necessarily politicized artists did not share *one single* vision of this project but rather produced individual approaches and ideas. One such form of cocreation and agency is often denied in retrospect to many artists working in the official spheres of the cultural world. On the other hand, judgment is strikingly unequal when works form other socialist, internationalist contexts are now added to the revised canon of Western art as emancipatory new discoveries while works form the GDR that are regarded as "conformist" are dismissed as mere propaganda. In the Cold War, both sides employed art as an ideological weapon.[6] These relationships must therefore be examined in a more differentiated way, also with regard to the declaration of political and cultural self-determination of African and Asian countries at the Bandung Conference in 1955.[7]

The Art of the GDR in the Global Context

The exhibition *Revolutionary Romances?* has many sister projects, and we refer to and build on their work. One should mention, for example, the research project *Decolonizing Socialism: Entangled Internationalism* at the Haute école d'art et de design (HEAD) in Geneva under the direction of Doreen Mende. It is studying artistic practices along a east–south axis of the socialist geographies of the Cold War.[8] A similar approach has been pursued by the research network *Multiple Artistic Mobilities—Travelling Artists from / to African Countries and European German-Speaking Countries* at the Universität Zürich.[9] The Museum der bildenden Künste in Leipzig opened the exhibition *Re-Connect. Art and Conflict in Brotherland* in May 2023, which primarily addressed the GDR history of immigration and the art work of immigrants before and after 1989/1990.[10] The Haus der Kulturen der Welt in Berlin dedicated a multidisciplinary program of exhibitions and events titled *Echoes of the Brother Countries* to the visions and illusions of antiimperialist solidarity.[11] These and other projects underscore the current interest in describing and analyzing the culture of the GDR in its global connections as well. Working with this theme has made it possible to develop new models for a differentiated approach to art from the GDR and to tie it to contemporary discourses on postcolonialism,

6   On this, see Anselm Franke, Nida Ghouse, Paz Guevara, and Antonia Majaca, eds., Parapolitics: Cultural Freedom and the Cold War, London 2021.

7   On this, see also ARTMargins 8 (2019), no. 2 (note 4).

8   https://entangledinternationalism.org/ (accessed on: 11.10.2023); see also the essay by Doreen Mende in this volume, p. 159–162.

9   https://www.khist.uzh.ch/de/chairs/moderne/forschung/mam.html (accessed on: 11.10.2023).

10   Re-Connect. Kunst und Kampf im Bruderland, ed. Marcus Hurttig, Sithara Weeratunga, exh. cat. Museum der bildenden Künste Leipzig, München 2023.

11   https://www.hkw.de/en/programme/echos-der-bruderlaender (accessed on: 11.10.2023).

racism, and ideological critique.[12] *Revolutionary Romances?* is unique because the exhibition is based primarily on research into the SKD's (own) holdings. In the context of the exhibitions theme, the history of its collection, including its omissions, categorizations, and even random qualities becomes evident. Previously unnoticed works are finally brought out of storage and bring forgotten or repressed stories to the public.

The exhibition was preceded by a series of research-based projects and events. As early as 2020, an issue of *Dresdener Kunstblätter* brought together initial results of research on the SKD collections.[13] A small research exhibition at the Albertinum in 2022 presented an exemplary selection of works on the theme.[14] It focused on the relationships between the GDR and Chile, Vietnam, Cuba, and South Africa. In parallel with that, contemporary artists were invited to reflection on this chapter of East German art history from the perspective of the present by intervening in the presentation of the Albertinum collection.[15] During the exhibition, the international conference *The Global GDR. A Transcultural History of Art, 1949–1990* was held at the Albertinum in June.[16] Some of the lectures of this conference have been included in this book. The annual program was concluded in the autumn of 2022 with the conference *Into the Cold. Alternative Artistic Trajectories into (Post-)Communist Europe.* Internationals scholars and curators as well as contemporary artists who work with postsocialist approaches, such as Slavs and Tatars, Jasmina Cibic, and Yevgeniy Fiks, presented different productive approaches to the difficulties of writing history after the Cold War.[17] *Voices,* the digital platform of SKD, had an accompanying film program curated by artists and curators such as Arlette Quỳnh-Anh Trần, Maria Berrios, and Mia Yu.

Last but not least, the research project *Art in Networks— The GDR and its Global Relations* represented a valuable resource for *Revolutionary Romances?* A group of young scholars supported by Europäischer Sozialfonds created a digital research platform under the direction of Kerstin Schankweiler at the Technische Universität Dresden in 2022 that presents international networks of artists, museums, and other cultural figures in the GDR.[18] In more than sixty video interviews, eyewitnesses, curators, and scholars relate their personal experiences, including critical and conflicting perspectives. Several of these interviews were integrated into the exhibition.

Carmelo González, Fraternal Countries, 1963, woodcut, 96 × 24 cm, Kupferstich-Kabinett, Staatliche Kunstsammlungen Dresden, inv. no. A 1965–216

12   On this, see also 1 Million Rosen für Angela Davis, ed. Staatliche Kunstsammlungen Dresden, Kathleen Reinhardt, Hilke Wagner, exh. cat. Kunsthalle im Lipsiusbau, Dresden, Milan 2020.

13   "Romantisch Revolutionär," special issue, Dresdener Kunstblätter 64 (2020), no. 3.

14   Revolutionary Romances. Transcultural Art Histories in the GDR | Prolog, Albertinum, Dresden, April 13–July 17, 2022 (extended until September 4, 2022).

15   It showed works and installations by Sung Tieu, Ângela Ferreira, Laura Horelli, and Emeka Ogboh.

16   Organized as a cooperation by the Technische Universität Dresden and the Albertinum of the Staatliche Kunstsammlungen Dresden, supported by the Fritz Thyssen Stiftung, Albertinum, Dresden, June 9–11, 2022, recording of the contributions: https://voices.skd.museum/en/voices-mag/the-global-gdr-a-transcultural-history-of-art-1949-1990/ (accessed on: 11.10.2023).

17   Supported by the Terra Foundation for American Art and the Goethe-Institut, Albertinum, Dresden, October 13, 2022, recording of the contributions: https://voices.skd.museum/en/voices-mag/revolutionary-romances-into-the-cold-alternative-trajectories-into-post-communist-europe/ (accessed on: 11.10.2023).

18   Project contributors: Pauline Hohn, Nora Kaschuba, Jule Lagoda, Elke Neumann, https://artinnetworks.webspace.tu-dresden.de/en (accessed on: 11.10.2023).

The Exhibition in the Albertinum

The exhibition at the Albertinum in Dresden approached the field of study outlined here in five chapters. More than two hundred works from the 1950s to the 1990s are on view, by artists from the GDR, Cuba, Chile, Vietnam, India, Iraq, Libya, Mozambique, and Burma (Myanmar), among other places. Setting out from the holdings of the SKD,[19] supplemented by selected loans, the exhibition looks at artist practice, the themes and motifs of real and alleged "revolutionary romances." The individual chapters are flanked by contemporary positions, some of which were commissioned. As a critical revision, they expand the field of themes and establish a connection to current issues.

The first chapter—*Ideals and Icons*—offers examples of how artists translated political and ideologically charged terms such as "solidarity" and "international friendship" into catchy visual expressions and at the same time contrasted with the Western imperialism as the picture of the enemy. The propaganda of this internationalism was always tied as well to the intellectual and political protagonists who lent the charisma to make these ideas persuasive. Their glorified portraits were a regular feature of the socialist production of images. Marx, Engels and Lenin (p. 33) represented the historical legacy in this context, contemporaries such as Fidel Castro, Angela Davis, Che Guevara, Patrice Lumumba, and Tamara Bunke personified the struggles of the present and a promising future. The chapter concludes with the work *Cultura Profiláctica* by the Cuban artist Hamlet Lavastida (b. 1983), whose paper cutouts include photos, logos, and symbols that refer to the repressive politics in Cuba, which still has a totalitarian government (p. 92/93), and hence comment critically on historical ideals and icons.

The second chapter is about the connection *Art and Solidarity.* In the conflicts of the Cold War, the GDR ceaselessly promoted its alliance with "peoples fighting for their freedom." Announcements of solidarity were omnipresent in everyday life in the GDR, their echo in the population positive, and the willing to donate considerable. But over the course of time, the idea of solidarity ossified from overuse by the media and the society in an empty ritual that for many people was depleted by the state-required monthly purchase of Soli-Marken (solidarity stamps) as clarified by Wenke Seemann (b. 1978) in her installation at the beginning of the exhibition (p. 108/109). In the art of the GDR, too, "solidarity" was omnipresent and the dividing line from propaganda fluid. Many artists worked on this theme because it received state support and promised exhibitions and sales. That did not rule out genuine feelings of solidarity and personal participation as motives. This chapter integrates the installation *Les étudiants africains et le Socialisme* by Georges Adéagbo (b. 1942), which addresses the GDR's relationship with socialist "brother countries" in Africa (p. 76/77). In her video *PLATTENLOTUS*, the Vietnamese artist Arlette Quỳnh-Anh Trần (b. 1987) speculates about the future of the city of Vinh, which was destroyed in the Vietnam War and then rebuilt as a socialist model city with support from the GDR (p. 114/115).

The headline of the third chapter is *Travels and Contacts.* The freedom to travel was strictly limited in the GDR. Like all cultural activities, travelling was subject to state bureaucracy and political control. It was often tied to arduous processes of application and arbitrary approval. Travels to friendly "brother countries" in Asia, Africa, and Latin America represented a great privilege. Whereas artists loyal to the system like Lea Grundig could travel the world extensively (p. 84), nonconformist artists had hardly any opportunities to make study trips to distant lands.[20] The exhibition shows examples of portraits and landscapes taken on trips by artists from the GDR to China, Cuba, Vietnam, and Cambodia. And if artists were not allowed to travel, their art could still overcome borders: East German

---

19   The majority of works shown are from the Kupferstich-Kabinett, the Kunstfonds, and the Albertinum of the SKD.
20   On opportunities for travel of East German artists, see also the essay by Nora Kaschuba, Jule Lagoda, and Kerstin Schankweiler in this volume, p. 147–152.

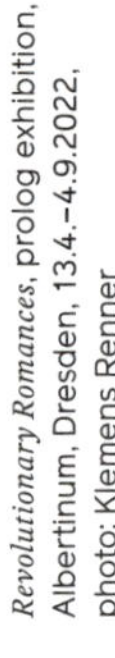

Revolutionary Romances, prolog exhibition, Albertinum, Dresden, 13.4.–4.9.2022, photo: Klemens Renner

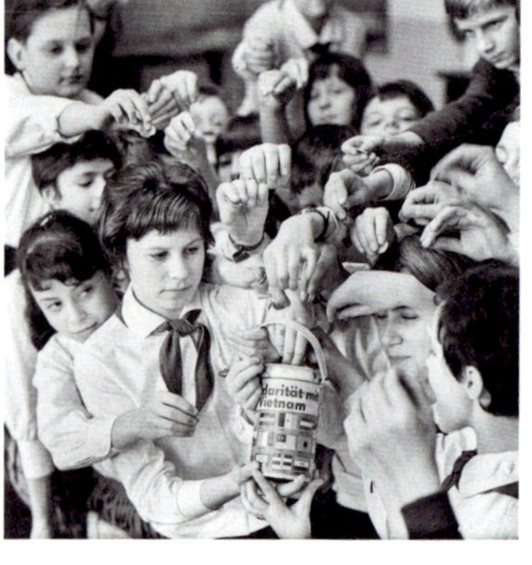

Fundraising of the Junge Pioniere (Young Pioneers, youth organisation of the GDR) for Vietnam, Dresden, 1966, photo: Erich Höhne & Erich Pohl

mail artists sent their works in postcard format into the world (p. 61) and were thus able to connect with an international network.[21] In her video *Geschmortes Herz* (Braised Heart), Sonya Schönberger (b. 1975) traces the trips of the "meritorious workers of the people" on the GDR cruise ship *MS Völkerfreundschaft* (p. 106). Sven Johne's (b. 1976) multipart photographic work is also about the rebuilt Vietnamese city of Vinh, which the author visited in 2008 and found in a state of "overgrown utopia" (p. 88/89).

From the early 1950s onward, people from many countries came to the GDR to study and work. The fourth chapter—*Temporary Guests?*—is dedicated to them. "Ausländerstudium" (study programs for foreigners) and "Arbeitskräftekooperation" (workforce cooperation) were considered living expressions of international friendship and were intended to help disseminate in the world a positive image of the GDR and of socialism. From 1949 to 1989/1990, around fifty students from Asia, Africa, and Latin America studied art at the Dresden Academy of Fine Arts. They came from China, Vietnam, Cambodia, Burma (Myanmar), Indonesia, Mongolia, Ethiopia, Mozambique, Iraq, Libya, Lebanon, Israel/Palestine, Brazil, Columbia, Syria, and Chile. The artists had to leave the GDR within four weeks of completing their studies. Only in exceptional cases—like the students from Chile who immigrated to the GDR after the military coup d'état in 1973—were they able to obtain permanent residence permits.

One example is the Palestinian artist Abed Abdi (b. 1942), who, with support from Lea Grundig, traveled from Haifa to the GDR in 1964 to study at the academy in Dresden. In 1966, his works were presented in the group exhibition *Gaststudenten in der Hochschule für Bildende Künste* (Visiting Students at the Academy of Fine Arts). As a student, Abdi also belonged to a group under the direction of Gerhard Bondzin that painted the iconic mural *Der Weg der Roten Fahne* (The Path of the Red Flag) at the Kulturpalast in Dresden in 1969. The Armenian-Lebanese artist Emmanuel Guiragossian (b. 1954) began studying in Dresden on a scholarship in 1974 and completed his degree with a thesis project of large-format oil paintings titled *Meine Schmerzen—Libanon* (My Pains—Lebanon), which dealt with the genocide of the Armenian people. During his time in Dresden, he was friends with A. R. Penck and still speaks of him with great admiration.[22] Martha Ketsela (b. 1955) of Ethiopia completed a six-month practical training at the academy in 1980, at the end of which she produced the print portfolio *Das Glück der Erde* (The Happiness of the Earth) (p. 90/91). The Chilean artist César Olhagaray (b. 1951) left his homeland after the military coup d'état, in the wake of which he had been imprisoned for a time. In Dresden, he began to study painting and printmaking in 1974 (p. 99). He was taught by, among others, Hernando Léon (b. 1933), who had himself studied in Dresden from 1958 to 1961 in Dresden and then lived

---

21 On the mail art exchange between the GDR and Latin America, see the essay by Elena Shtromberg in this volume, p. 49–55.
22 Interview with Emmanuel Guiragossian, June 22, 2022: https://artinnetworks.webspace.tu-dresden.de/de/beitraege/ein-kuenstlerleben-zwischen-beirut-dresden-und-berlin (accessed on: 18.10.2023).

in Chile before being forced to leave the country after the coup. He returned to Dresden with his wife, the artist Margarita Pellegrin (p. 102/103), and was a lecturer at the academy from 1974 to 1992 (p. 165). Despite what these examples might lead one to assume, this chapter of the international students at the Dresden Academy of Fine Arts has yet to be studied in depth. A first approach is offered by the interviews with former students that are presented in this chapter of the exhibition. A small selection of their student and thesis works are also being shown for the first time. They are testimony to the diversity of the art scene of the GDR, which usually plays no role in art historical studies and seems to be almost forgotten.

The image conveyed to the public of the daily lives of students and contract workers was harmonious. Officially, they were treated as equals of the citizens of the GDR, but they were in fact disadvantaged in many respects. That was true not least of their private lives. Personal contacts outside of their studies and work were undesirable and love affairs with citizens of the GDR not on the agenda—nevertheless, true romances did occur. One Vietnamese contract worker's plan to marry a woman from Dresden that was thwarted by the authorities is the focus of a new installation that Sung Tieu (b. 1987) developed especially for the exhibition (p. 110/111). Even though "temporary guests" were not really integrated into GDR society, they were often in demand as models for East German painters. Numerous portraits of people from other countries and cultures reflect the "tiny" GDR's desire for internationality and cosmopolitanism. Although these portraits show specific people, they also reflect stereotypical perspectives (p. 19, 36, 107). They emphasize their obvious "otherness" in the East German milieu and exoticize the sitters. Extremely generalizing titles such as *Afrikanischer Student* (African Student) and *Afrikanische Freundinnen* (African Friends) ignore the individual in favor of superficial, Eurocentric categorization. The two-channel-video projection *Re-Writing Gaze* by Dana Lorenz (b. 1984) responds to our pigeon-holing look at five protagonists and thus exposes the power structure of seeing and being seen (p. 96/97).

Another part of the cultural exchange with the Global South was extensive exhibition activity. The GDR had not only large historical exhibitions on art from Mexico, Nigeria, and China but also many presentations of contemporary art from Asia, Africa, and Latin America. This presence raises the question of whether this art was also collected by museums in the GDR. The final chapter—*Collected 'Fraternally'?*—explores this issue using the example of several works from the holdings of the SKD. The collection of the Albertinum has several paintings by artists from India (p. 34), Iraq (p. 73), Burma (Myanmar, p. 59), Indonesia, Cuba, and North Korea. These works were not, however, actively acquired by the museum but entered the collection as bequests and gifts or were transferred to the Albertinum by the Ministry of Culture. In the GDR era, art from countries of the Global South was not a focus of the museum's collecting or research, and even today these works, their themes, their motifs, and the biographies of their artists have yet to be studied adequately.

Permadi Lyosta, Dune Landscape, oil on canvas, 85 × 120.5 cm, Albertinum, Staatliche Kunstsammlungen Dresden, Gal.-no. 3556
The painting by the Indonesian artist was transferred to the Albertinum by the Ministry of Culture of the GDR in 1963.

Looking Ahead

After a first heyday in the 1990s, the history of the GDR has been receiving more attention again in literature, theater, contemporary art, and scholarship. Critical engagement with the GDR had, of course, never vanished completely from the public sphere or scholarly research. It may, however, be related to generational change and greater distance that young people in particular are showing an interest in exploring the history of the land of the Sozialistische Einheitspartei Deutschland (SED; Socialist Unity Party of Germany) within a broader context. This change in viewpoint has shifted focus to themes that had previously been treated only on the margins and are characterized by feminist and decolonial approaches but are being reflected on more broadly in our neoliberal present. It is imperative that the focus within the field of the visual arts in the GDR shift as well: From the 1990s onward, the debate focused on the "Bilderstreit" (picture controversy) and hence on the relationship between the two Germanys,[23] but now transnational connections and an internally differentiated perspective on cultural diversity are being explored.

Revolutionary Romances? combines the works of art and other documents of a failed utopia of real socialism with the desire for more multifaceted looks at art (hi)stories today. The differentiated, self-critical gaze using the example of the Dresden State Art Collections therefore not only testifies to curiosity about its complexities and involvements but also marks new fields of study that bring with them the challenges of our present.

23   Karl-Siegbert Rehberg and Paul Kaiser, eds.: Bilderstreit und Gesellschaftsumbruch. Die Debatten um die Kunst aus der DDR im Prozess der deutschen Wiedervereinigung, Berlin/Kassel 2013; Kathleen Reinhardt: Can the Artists Help Survive? New Approaches to Art of the GDR, Looking Back while Moving Forward (2019): http://mezosfera.org/can-the-artists-help-survive-new-approaches-to-art-of-the-gdr-looking-back-while-moving-forward/ (accessed on: 15.11.2023).

Trịnh Kim Vinh (right), professor Gerhard Kettner (left), and the printer Roland Erhardt (middle) in the lithography workshop of the Dresden Academy of Fine Arts, 1973
Trịnh Kim Vinh studied 1971–1973 at the Academy of Fine Arts in Dresden.

Hartmut Henschel, Chile 1973, 1974, screen print, 59.7 × 42 cm, Kunstfonds,
Staatliche Kunstsammlungen Dresden, inv. no. L 06432

Raúl Martínez, Lenin, 1970, film poster, color screen print, 58.5 × 43.5 cm, Kupferstich-Kabinett, Staatliche Kunstsammlungen Dresden, inv. no. A 2020-16

Kattingeri Krishna Hebbar, The Evening, 1967, oil on canvas, 76 × 88.5 cm, Albertinum, Staatliche Kunstsammlungen Dresden, Gal. no. 3856

The selection, which was made by the Ministry, had no focal points. It was a mixture of different genres, of different ways of making art. [...] There was also no regional focus. The center had no influence on the selection—it had to make do with what came in. The quality of what came from abroad was actually quite good and, particularly for visitors in the GDR, it always possessed a certain 'exoticism', because it was often art that didn't fit into the official canon of GDR art or the understanding of art— not at all. But it was done because the GDR wanted to show everyone: look how cosmopolitan we are.

Peter Hartmann on the exhibitions of art from abroad, organized by the Zentrum für Kunstausstellungen der DDR (Center for Art Exhibitions of the GDR) in East Berlin and other East German cities, interview as part of the research project *Art in Networks—The GDR and its Global Relations*, see p. 171.

Eva Schulze-Knabe, Liang Yun-chin (Chinese art student), 1959, oil on canvas, 105 × 80 cm, Kunstfonds, Staatliche Kunstsammlungen Dresden, inv. no. 192/80
Liang Yun-chin studied 1956–1961 at the Academy of Fine Arts in Dresden.

Christian Saehrendt

The Foreign Cultural Policy of East Germany in the Global South: Fine Art on Behalf of a "Socialist World System"

"The Socialist World System, the international proletariat, and the national liberation movements flow together into a powerful stream and determine the main direction of historical development."[1]

For decades, a global geopolitical confrontation of blocs like that of the Cold War appeared to be a historical episode that had ended: the West under the leadership of the United States against a Socialist World System whose backbone was formed by the USSR. Since the spring of 2022, however, the world has once again split along this historical fracture line. The Socialist World System has returned as an anti-Western international alliance, but now entirely without socialist ideology and focused on military cooperation and trading in raw materials.[2] This became clear after the Russian invasion of Ukraine and the Western policy of sanctions that followed, in which Africa and Asia hardly participate at all. In addition, China, which is still officially communist, is showing sympathy and support for Russia. As a result, it has become impossible to overlook the great influence that Russia once again has in Asia and Africa, in large part because the elites that were educated prior to 1990 and are now in power in numerous countries of the Global South tend to be pro-socialist. In these often-superannuated autocratic regimes, there are still many graduates of Soviet universities and party-run schools. Moreover, the Russian regime has strengthened its relations to Africa and the Middle East over the past fifteen years. China's influence on the Global South is even stronger, having achieved it through economic cooperation and seemingly generous loans. In several countries such as the People's Republic of the Congo, China had already established a foothold during the Cold War and was competing with the Soviet Union there at the time.

As many colonies were becoming independent in the 1950s and 1960s, the Eastern Bloc had a historical opportunity to export its own social system to the South and thus truly become a Socialist World System and have achieve strategical superiority over the West in the long term. The German Democratic Republic operated as a junior partner of the USSR and provided extensive aid to the development of the state, the economy, and infrastructure in these new nations. Long-term influence on the new elites of these states was to be ensured not only through support and collaboration in the areas of technology, state security, economy, and administration but also through the export of science, culture, and ideology. Art, education, and Marxist schooling were instruments of foreign policy for the GDR. Exhibition exchanges, scholarship programs, and aid to build new academies of art were instruments of a policy whose goal was to consolidate and progressively integrate a Socialist

---

1   *Woche der Solidarität mit den um ihre Befreiung kämpfenden Völkern in Mosambik, Angola und Guinea* in der DDR, Oktober 1972. Redebeiträge und Materialien (contributions and materials), Bundesarchiv Berlin-Lichterfelde (BArch), DZ 8 no. 204.

2   Mercenaries from the Wagner Group have been active in, among other places, in Syria, Sudan, Mozambique, and Mali—countries that had initially or temporarily been Socialist-oriented. See Marat Gabidullin: Wagner. Putins geheime Armee. Ein Insiderreport, Berlin 2022, p. 30–31. In the Central African Republic, the group received mining rights for diamonds and gold in exchange for its services (Andrea Böhm and Michael Thumann: Putins bester Schurke, in: Die Zeit, February 9, 2023, p. 6). The Russian navy conducted maneuvers with South Africa off the coast in the Indian Ocean (Christian Putsch: Russland weitet seinen Einfluss in Südafrika aus, in: Neue Zürcher Zeitung, February 13, 2023, p. 6), while in Johannesburg Russia Today established its first station in Africa. See Christoph Plate: Putins Propagandaoffensive in Afrika: https://www.zeit.de/politik/ausland/2022-08/russland-afrika-propaganda-wladimir-putin (accessed on: 9.8.2022).

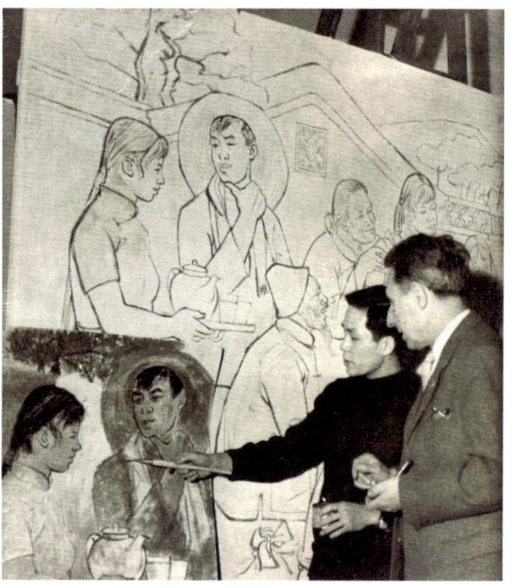

World System. On the one hand, the GDR was trying thus to have sustainable and long-term influence on the economic policies of the new nation-states to obtain raw materials and markets for its goods. On the other hand, its demonstrative internationalism could also improve its image and assert its importance in international politics. This may have been linked to a hope for a "charisma transfer": The GDR, whose bureaucracy became rigid early on, imagined itself as a young nation, and the Moscow-dependent SED (Socialist Unity Party of Germany) as a German antiimperialist liberation movement, in a front with the young nation-states of Africa and Asia, fraternally united in a struggle against the old colonial powers and their racism. The popular revolutionary leaders of the South such as Fidel Castro, Che Guevara, Ho Chi Minh, and Samora Machel but also the American civil rights activist Angela Davis were heroes with whom the Politburo could present itself advantageously.

Among the regions on which the foreign cultural policy of the GDR focused, in addition to Asia and Latin America, were the former Portuguese colonies in Africa and the countries of the Middle East. Some examples of this cultural work are highlighted below. When Portugal's colonial empire collapsed after more than four centuries, it triggered a geopolitical battle over its legacy, in which the Eastern Bloc emerged as a winner for a time. Angola and Mozambique, both of which became independent in 1975, were especially close allies of the Soviet Union and the GDR, which in turn were particularly engaged there. The GDR had already supported the liberation struggle on various levels in these countries. The physician and poet António Agostinho Neto (1922–1979), a founding member and the chairman of the MPLA (Movimento Popular de Libertação de Angola), became Angola's first president. He had recently visited the GDR. Because oil deliveries from the Soviet Union were constantly increasing in price, the GDR was trying to establish other sources of raw materials and energy. Angola had the potential to become an important trading partner in that respect. The volume of foreign trade of both countries rose rapidly already the same year. A close network of relations between the political parties and state organizations of the two countries was established; many delegations from Berlin and Luanda visited each other.[3] A delegation from the GDR was present at the very first MLPA Party Conference in 1977. Under the leadership of Neto's successor, José Eduardo dos Santos, Angola relied

---

3   Johannes Kuppe: Teure Freunde. Zum Staatsbesuch von Angolas Staatspräsident in der DDR, in: Deutschland Archiv 11 (1981), p. 1130–1133, here p. 1130–1031.

increasingly on the Eastern Bloc and remained dependent because a protracted civil war was raging in the country.[4] The GDR collaborated with the southern African country on a cultural level as well. Art from Angola was presented in the GDR several times. While Erich Honecker was in Luanda on a state visit,[5] the exhibition *Angola: Traditionelle Kunst – Kunst der Gegenwart* (Angola: Traditional Art—Contemporary Art) at the Museum für Völkerkunde (Museum of Ethnology) in Dresden in the spring of 1979 offered a survey of the history of the country's art.[6] The museum offered a platform to art from Africa and Asia regularly.[7] According to the GDR press, the sculptures, metalworks, and paintings testify to the "diverse efforts to preserve carefully Angola's national cultural heritage and to develop a revolutionary culture."[8] A cultural historical exhibition with 750 artifacts from all periods from antiquity to the presents, ranging from tools and household items to art ("from the camel bell to the propaganda poster") from Angola, Mozambique, and Ethiopia was held at the Ausstellungszentrum am Fernsehturm in Berlin (Exhibition Center at the Berlin Television Tower) in the autumn of 1980.[9] In 1981, on the occasion of a state visit form President Dos Santos in the GDR, a working plan for cultural and scientific cooperation was signed to enhance the partnership of the two countries.[10]

The Portuguese colony Mozambique had declared independence in 1975 and proclaimed itself a People's Republic. In February 1979, Erich Honecker visited Mozambique after Angola and signed a treaty on friendship and economic cooperation. The following year, in the province of Niassa, skilled workers from East Germany began one of the largest agricultural developmental aid projects in Africa. As noted above, the GDR was interested in securing alternative sources of raw materials and energy in Angola and Mozambique. The economic integration of these countries into the structure of the socialist economic alliance COMECON (Council for Mutual Economic Assistance) proved to be of great use in that respect, although considerably preliminary work and investments were necessary. Whereas oil production was of interest in Angola, in Mozambique the goal was to obtain rights for opencast mining because it was believed that the Moatize mining district had the largest anthracite deposits in Africa. Coal was mined in the area from 1977, largely under the direction of the GDR; the coal output was to be divided evenly between the two countries. Experts from the GDR set up a medical base and a rescue service for the miners, and local managers and foremen received several dozen prefabricated homes from the GDR. A canteen, school and a kindergarten were also built. In 1980, a cultural and social center and a cinema followed. Moatize thus became a socialist model city on African soil.[11] In 1982, the East German developmental aid worker Harald Heinke and the Mozambican artist Mankew Valente Mahumane (1934–2021) produced a large mural at the Moatize Cultural Center depicting miners from Mozambique and East Germany working together.[12] In this way, cultural work flanked the economic relationships of the two countries. The Mozambican Ministry of Education and Culture also temporarily employed GDR advisors who were tasked with working on a new education system for the 'socialist man' in Africa.

4   In 1976 along, the GDR provided weapons and financial assistance totaling 107 million deutschmark. See Hermann Wentker: Außenpolitik in engen Grenzen. Die DDR im internationalen System, Munich 2007, p. 462–463.

5   Erich Honecker und Agostinho Neto: DDR und Angola brüderlich verbunden, in: Neues Deutschland, February 19, 1979, p. 1.

6   *Angola: Traditionelle Kunst – Kunst der Gegenwart*, Museum für Völkerkunde, Dresden, February 24–March 25, 1979, afterwards in Budapest. Bundesarchiv Berlin-Lichterfelde (BArch) DR 123 no. 118.

7   "As a rule, cooperations with nonaligned countries were mediated by the Ministry of Higher and Technical Education (to which the Museum of Ethnology in Dresden, as a research institution, reported at the time), the Ministry of Culture, or the Center for Art Exhibitions of the DDR." Information from Petra Martin, curator of the State Ethnographic Collections of Saxony, to the author, e-mail, November 17, 2016.

8   ADN news item, in: Die Neue Zeit, February 24, 1979, p. 8.

9   Ausstellungszentrum am Fernsehturm, October 1–26, 1980, Bundesarchiv Berlin-Lichterfelde (BArch) DR 123 no. 143.

10   Kuppe 1981 (note 3), p. 1132.

11   See Rostende Erbstücke aus DDR-Zeiten, in: Neue Zürcher Zeitung, August 23, 2002: https://www.nzz.ch/article8CI86-ld.221414 (accessed on: 18.4.2023).

12   Harald Heinke: Mankeu Valente Mahumane – über den künstlerischen Lebensweg des mosambikanischen Malers, in: INDABA. Das SADOCC-Magazin für das südliche Afrika 66 (2010), p. 20–25, here p. 22.

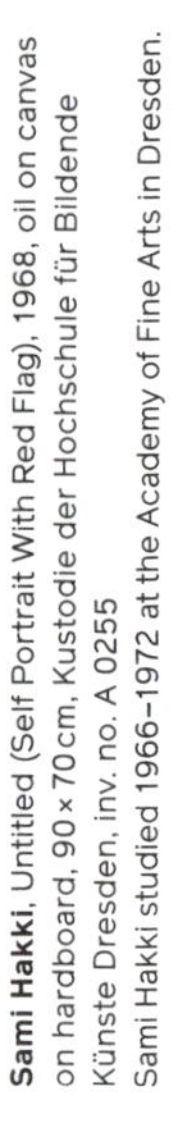

Cultural exchange with African and Arab countries was a state matter, but it was also based significantly on the personal commitment of individuals who made friendships while traveling abroad and who advocated artistic collaboration. The East German developmental aid worker and amateur painter Harald Heinke lived in Mozambique from 1979 to 1985. He took numerous photographs of his everyday impressions there and became friends with the painter Mankew Valente Mahumane, who was very famous in Mozambique.[13] Wolfgang Eckardt (1919–1999) was another of the individuals committed to starting an artistic dialogue between the two countries.[14] The sculptor, who had created the memorial to revolutionary sailors for the municipal port in Rostock, collected donations to buy tools for wood-carvers in Mozambique.[15] At his own expense, with support from the Fischkombinat Rostock (Rostock Fish Collective Combine) and the Verband Bildender Künstler (VBK; Association of Visual Artists) of the GDR, he traveled to Mozambique three times to cultivate contacts with artists such as Mankew. In 1982, Eckardt visited a Makonde village near Pemba: "There he sat on the ground in the circle of hosts. They explained their carving technique to him, and he showed them how we do it", read an East German press report. At the time, Eckardt had traveled by jeep 1500 kilometers into the interior of the country. In 1987, he exhibited in Maputo, including sculptures inspired by his two previous trips, as well as a portrait of President Samora Machel, who had died the previous year. Four thousand visitors saw this exhibition, Eckardt recalled: "After the opening, I saw again and again that people picked up the sculptures to hold—an unfamiliar sight for us."[16] Mozambican artists visited Eckardt in Rostock, including Mankew, who came to the GDR in 1984 at the invitation of the Liga für Völkerfreundschaft (International Friendship League). The painter and ceramicist Noel Langa (b. 1938) and his brother Naftal Langa (1932–2014), a sculptor, exhibited at the Kunsthalle Rostock in the spring of 1988. Eckardt's wife, Ilse-Dore Eckardt, described their meetings with fellow artists from Mozambique as always cordial and easygoing.[17]

13   Ibid.
14   Protokoll der Beratung der Freundschaftsgesellschaft DDR-VRM (minutes of the consultation of the GDR-Vietnam friendship society), November 28, 1986, Bundesarchiv Berlin-Lichterfelde (BArch) DY 13 no. 3068.
15   Horst-Dieter Seffner: Garnelen und Maipapa vor Südafrika, in: Wir haben Spuren hinterlassen. Die DDR in Mosambik, ed. Matthias Voß, Münster 2005, p. 314–318, here p. 317.
16   Wolfgang Eckardt: Schnitzeisen nach Maputo, in: Der Sonntag, August 28, 1988, p. 24.
17   Ilse-Dore Eckardt in conversation with the author, April 8, 2016.

In 1978, the Ministry of Foreign Affairs in East Berlin compiled a list of fifteen non-European states that it classified as "socialist-oriented" and with which more intensive relationships were to be established. The criteria were an at least partially nationalized economy, a sector of the economy based on cooperatives, and a leading cadre party. In the Middle east, the GDR had been concentrating on Syria and Iraq since the mid-1950s, and these relationships were to be strengthened in the coming years. The pan-Arab and left-wing ideas of the nationalist Ba'ath Party, which was popular among young members of the military and urban elites in the Middle East, offered the GDR several promising points of ideological connection. The regimes in Damascus and Baghdad were, however, less interested in importing Marxist ideology and focused instead on establishing pragmatic development dictatorships. The Soviet Union and the GDR attempted to exert long-term influence on the Arab elites not only through technological and economic aid, but also through culture and education. Syria had been a focus of GDR cultural policy already since the late 1950s, with regard to both education and fine art. Reciprocal visits by artists to the partner countries and exhibitions were organized and advice and assistance with developing cultural centers and art schools in Syria was provided. The Syrian artists and the Arab public were to be shaped in the spirit of Socialist Realism and inspired to create decidedly political art. The developmental aid of the GDR ran into diverse obstacles in Syria; sometimes it also lacked competent developmental aid workers. In 1966, for example, a guest lecturer was to be sent to the University of Damascus to accelerate the development of the art academy. The Syrian government offered a good monthly salary but could not find anyone at the Academy of Fine Arts in Dresden with adequate knowledge of English or French.[18] With the opening of the Cultural and Information Center of the GDR in Damascus, the cultural presence of the GDR was institutionalized. A first assessment at the middle of the year 1968 already listed 132 events with 33,000 visitors, but the center cooperated with Syrian cultural institutions, and most of those events had taken place outside of the center.[19] Official cultural relations between Syria and the GDR reached a high point in 1987 when the Berlin painter and director of the Art Academy in East Berlin Walter Womacka (1925–2010) was commissioned with a portrait of President Hafez al-Assad.[20]

The GDR also had close relationships with neighboring Iraq as well, which was ruled by a wing of the Ba'ath Party that was hostile to Damascus. Iraq had been one of the first states to recognize the GDR. The Ba'ath Party first came to power in Baghdad in 1963; in retrospect, it referred to its seizure of power as a 'socialist revolution'.[21] Saddam Hussein ruled as a dictator from 1979 onward. Despite considerable political differences and a certain unreliability of the regime in Baghdad, considerable cultural exchange between the countries developed from the mid-1960s and reached its peak in 1978, shortly before the beginning of Saddam's autocratic rule. With the opening of a cultural and information center in Baghdad in 1968, culture from the GDR had a fixed place of representation in Iraq. In the following years there was a rapid succession of reciprocal exhibitions.[22] Its cultural partnership with the GDR was part of the Ba'ath Party's plan to make Iraq a modern Arab hegemonic power on all levels and to accumulate international prestige. During the First Gulf War (1980–1988), cultural exchange waned. Despite declining opportunities to exert ideological and political influence, the GDR maintained relations with Saddam Husseins's dictatorship until the end.

---

18   Request from the Ministry of Culture to the HfBK Dresden, June 3, 1966, rejection by the HfBK, June 28, 1966, Archiv HfBK Dresden 03/0073.

19   Bericht über die Veranstaltungstätigkeit im ersten Halbjahr (report on event activities in the first half of 1968), June 26, 1968, Bundesarchiv Berlin-Lichterfelde (BArch) DY 13 no. 2091.

20   Walter Womacka: Farbe bekennen. Erinnerungen, Berlin 2004, p. 244.

21   Arab Socialist Ba'ath Party, Revolutionary Iraq, 1968–1973. The Political Report. Adopted by the Eighth Regional Congress of the Arab Ba'th Socialist Party-Iraq, Baghdad, 1974 (English translation by the Iraqi Ministry of Information), p. 129 and 220.

22   Vereinbarung über die Zusammenarbeit vom VBK und der Gewerkschaft der Künstler der Republik Irak 1986–88 (agreement on cooperation between the GDR's Artists' Association and the Union of Artists of the Republic of Iraq), March 18, 1986, Archiv Stiftung Akademie der Künste Berlin (AdK), VBK ZV no. 458.

In summary, it can be said that the GDR undertook considerable efforts, given its limited resources, to enter cultural relations with countries of the Global South. There was often only a time window of a maximum of ten to fifteen years to do so. There was a lively exchange of cultural delegations, a large number of reciprocal art exhibitions, and a number of African and Arab graduates from GDR art schools such as Sami Hakki (b. 1945), who got to know both cultures and had the potential to build bridges between the two partner countries. In Africa and the Middle East, the GDR's cultural relationships to Syria, Iraq, and the Palestinian Liberation Organization (PLO) in Beirut were particularly close, followed by Ethiopia, Angola, and Mozambique. Contacts with Tanzania, Somalia, Ghana, Mali, Guinea, and several other countries were more sporadic. As a rule, cultural exchange took place between state, political, or communal organizations. Lasting cooperation between art schools, such as student exchanges, reciprocal guest lectures, or harmonization of curricula only took place to a limited exent possibly due to bureaucratic obstacles and a lack of resources. In places, were hardly any state structures existed, cultural exchange was in the hands of individual committed artists who also established international personal friendships. It should be remembered, however, that cultural policy was not the priority in the relations between real socialism and the young nations of Africa and Asia but rather had flanking and decorative functions—economic and security policy stood clearly in the foreground. The stability of these security policy and economic ties is particularly evident today, when Russia—or rather its mercenary company PMC Wagner—is once again present in many former socialist countries in Africa and the Middle East and African countries are seeking proximity to Russia for economic reasons. By contrast, cultural policy left behind less visible traces. Today, it is difficult to identify successes and lasting effects of the GDR's cultural policy in Africa and the Middle East. The time frame in most cases was too short, and the general circumstances too hostile to culture because civil wars, economic plight, and scarcity of resource pushed cultural work down the list of priorities of the countries involved. Regulated cultural exchange that also reached the provinces and the broader public of the African and Middle Eastern countries involved was something for times of peace— and they were long in coming. As a result, the ideologically and state-motivated foreign cultural policy of the GDR left its deepest traces in the personal and individual: in the artist friendship that developed and in the biographies of those who were able to study or exhibit in the GDR.

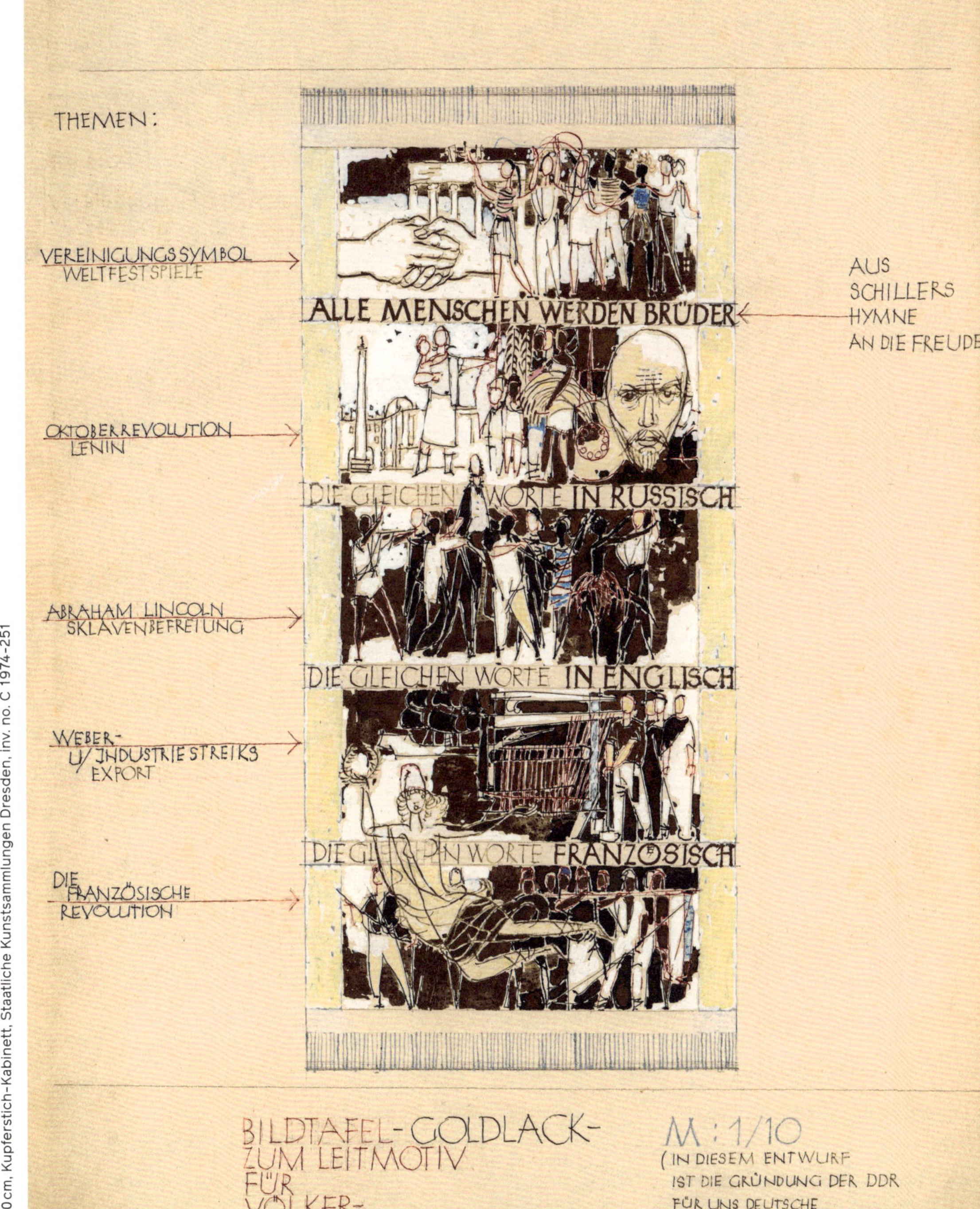
THEMEN:
VEREINIGUNGS SYMBOL
WELTFESTSPIELE
AUS
SCHILLERS
HYMNE
AN DIE FREUDE
ALLE MENSCHEN WERDEN BRÜDER
OKTOBERREVOLUTION
LENIN
DIE GLEICHEN WORTE IN RUSSISCH
ABRAHAM LINCOLN
SKLAVENBEFREIUNG
DIE GLEICHEN WORTE IN ENGLISCH
WEBER-
U/ JNDUSTRIE STREIKS
EXPORT
DIE GLEICHEN WORTE FRANZÖSISCH
DIE
FRANZÖSISCHE
REVOLUTION
BILDTAFEL-GOLDLACK-
ZUM LEITMOTIV
FÜR
VÖLKER-
VERSTÄNDIGUNG
M : 1/10
(IN DIESEM ENTWURF
IST DIE GRÜNDUNG DER DDR
FÜR UNS DEUTSCHE
DIE KRÖNUNG
DER HISTORISCHEN ENTWICKLLUNG)

H. Kessler, Solidarity, 1973, light metal, etched, 3 parts, left panel: 59.5 × 85.5 × 6.3 cm, centre panel: 79.5 × 59.7 × 9 cm, right panel: 53.8 × 60 × 6.3 cm, Kunstfonds, Staatliche Kunstsammlungen Dresden, inv. no. L 03458

Johannes Heisig, A Mistake (for Eugen in Pretoria), 1987, mixed media on canvas, 190 × 270 cm, Albertinum, Staatliche Kunstsammlungen Dresden, inv. no. 88/21

The 80s brought great success for GDR art abroad, because a generation of young artists was dominant, who produced very attractive art. This led to major discussions within the country and was received abroad as interesting art coming from the GDR, which had not been expected. And this strengthened the image of GDR art enormously in the 80s. This led to tensions internally and increased recognition of GDR art on the outside.

The art historian Hans-Jörg Schirmbeck on exhibitions with art from the GDR abroad, interview as part of the research project *Art in Networks—The GDR and its Global Relations*, see p. 171.

Leonhard Frank Duch, mail art to Robert Rehfeldt, 1975, card with stamps and handwriting, 7.6 × 10.5 cm, mail art Archive of Ruth Wolf-Rehfeldt and Robert Rehfeldt

Elena
Shtromberg

The Global Postal[1]

I want to begin by presenting a rather unusual object, a postcard, sent as part of an ongoing mail art exchange between the artists Leonhard Frank Duch (b. 1940) in Brazil and Robert Rehfeldt (1931–1993) in the German Democratic Republic (GDR). A cursory observation of Duch's postcard identifies it as a tourist souvenir from Itamaraca, an island just off the coast of Recife, the city in the north of Brazil where the artist was living. What immediately emerges is the word "KUNST", stamped brightly in red across the contents of the card, acting as a bureaucratic seal identifying the piece as a work of art. At the center of the card is an object that is not instantly recognizable until one reads the accompanying text along the bottom, "The skin of my sunburnt thigh in itamaraca" as well as the handwritten words, "Souvenir from Itamaraca". It is both humorous and puzzling prompting the recipient to examine the details further. Itamaraca is an island just off the coast of Recife, ostensibly a place where one vacations and gets exposed to too much sun and thus gets sunburnt. The many allusions to a holiday contained in this greeting take an unusual if not perverse turn with the recognition that actual dead skin belonging to the artist is attached to the center of the postcard, stamped below with the word "VIVA" (alive). The tranquility of a beach vacation is now complicated by the almost forensic quality of the skin attached, a disturbing physical trace of the artist. The curious communique is further compounded when one learns that Itamaraca, a beautiful and isolated beach, as the artist described it, was also the site of the Barreto Campelo, a military prison from 1973 to 1979, where those accused of challenging the military regime would have landed. The postcard now piques the receivers' curiosity, foiling expectations and certainly complicating the myth of a holiday in a Brazilian tropical paradise. Here the skin, detached from the human body, intimates death or harm, a discomfort surely felt by the recipient, whom Duch had never met in person, as he comes into intimate contact with this piece of the sender's body on the other side of the world.

The artist Leonhard Frank Duch was born in Berlin in 1940 and immigrated to Brazil in 1951 where he attended art school and became a prominent member of the mail art network.[2] During the 1970s, a decade marked by the military dictatorship in Brazil, he was among a small group of artists to first engage in mail art, an international system of communication that to a large extent existed outside of government control and vigilance and certainly outside of the art market.[3] Acting as an unofficial artistic circuit, mail art allowed artists living in authoritarian regimes to express socially critical and anti-government positions in graphically creative, conceptually inventive ways, that would otherwise have been sanctioned. More importantly, it allowed artists to send their work anywhere the post office could reach, so while there were many restrictions on where the artists themselves could physically travel, their work could reach across multiple borders. Ironically, the post office, a social system administered by the government and known for the heavy-handed application of State bureaucracy instead facilitated an inexpensive and alternative forum for illicit exchange. Mail artists comprised sizeable networks of artists and recipients, many of whom came from different countries in Latin America, Asia and Europe, all representing vastly different social and political systems. The unique nature of this network did not make it unusual that Duch reached Ruth Wolf-Rehfeldt (b. 1932) and Robert Rehfeldt, the artist couple living in East Berlin who cultivated a robust network of exchange which included

---

1   The title of this essay is based on a stamp art project led by Ed Varney in Vancouver in 1984.
2   For more on Duch's life see the interview with author: http://www.thirdtext.org/schtromberg-duch (accessed on: 21.4.2023).
3   It is only in the last few years that these communiques have become something museums and collectors consider worthy of attention.

Latin American artists. In fact, Duch's first experience with mail art in 1975 included Robert Rehfeldt, when he received and responded to a chain letter on which a number of addresses and artist names were printed, among them that of Robert, who responded promptly.[4] Robert and his wife Ruth were well known for their activities with mail art and in 1975 Robert organized the first (and several after) mail art exhibition in the GDR, many of which took place at the Galerie Arkade in East Berlin. These exhibits were later documented in self-made publications, printed and xeroxed as a zine might be, then sent to the involved participants and other interested parties, in Latin America and elsewhere. The wide global reach of this network makes it an early harbinger of the kinds of communication circuits later made possible by the Internet. Within the context of the exhibition *Revolutionary Romances?* which seeks to display the global sphere of influence initiated by the GDR, mail art provides a unique lens for examining the network of exchange with Latin America, particularly during the 1970s and 1980s, the peak of mail art activity. In this essay, I offer brief glances at several of the many nodes in this constellation that signaled a rich exchange of art as correspondence signaling official and unofficial connections forged between East German and Latin American artists, providing a platform for further critical and scholarly pursuits.

Mail art was one of many media, including posters and prints, that comprised a robust exchange of graphic art between Latin America and the GDR. One prominent, official example of such an exchange was the triennial *INTERGRAFIK*, held from 1965–1990, and sponsored by the Solidaritätskomittee der DDR (GDR Solidarity Committee), in which international artists from around the world would participate with works that incorporated the theme of peace, as is well detailed in Annabel Ruckdeschel's essay for this catalogue.[5] While the iconography surrounding solidarity and liberation was widely, if not excessively deployed throughout the *INTERGRAFIK* exhibitions, there was also quite a bit of innovation on display achieved through unique experimentation with poetry and graphic conventions. One example that stands out is a poster by Klaus Storde (b. 1947) from 1978, which has the word "CHILE" spelled out with the colors of its flag, with the word "*HILF*" (Help!) embedded into text the in a way that communicates danger.[6] Posters were prominently represented in the graphic exchanges between the two regions, some of them announcing revolutionary films or events in places like Cuba, Mexico, and Nicaragua, later circulating in the GDR.[7]

The unofficial graphic exchange between these distinct regions initiated through the mail art network in a wide variety of formats leads one to explore a whole range of political and personal relationships that originated from within the domestic space and made their way across international borders through the postal system. As such, mail art is a lens into a mode of relay and communication that successfully navigated the complex boundaries initiated by politically enforced restrictions on public expression, thus evading strict censorship measures that were rigorously applied to other artistic media.

Like the existing graphic propositions in *INTERGRAFIK*, mail artworks often alluded to political repression and the difficulties of being an artist living in an authoritarian society. In a postcard by Duch, you see the artist standing behind bars with a big red stamp announcing, "I am an Artist".[8] The work presents the recipient with multiple interpretations, among them the suggestion that being an artist is comparable to living in prison; another is the plea that he has done nothing wrong and that he is simply an artist; or even a more

4 Interview with author July 14, 2022.
5 See p. 133–139 in this volume.
6 At this time Chile was ruled by a military junta led by the dictator Augusto Pinochet after a coup d'état in 1973. His regime was extremely hostile to anything it deemed subversive by the people of Chile.
7 For more on GDR posters in Latin America, including Klaus Storde's *Chile! Hilf*, see the virtual exhibit *Transnational Poster Art: Former East Germany (GDR) and Latin America 1970–1989* available through Stanford Libraries at: https://web.stanford.edu/~nauerbac/ddr%20kunst_exhibit_sept10/exhibit/GDRposters/posterart.html (accessed on: 21.4.2023).
8 Work in artist's personal archive. For similar examples see Jorge Bucksdricker, ed.: I AM AN ARTIST: Leonhard Frank Duch e a Arte Correio, Florianópolis 2020.

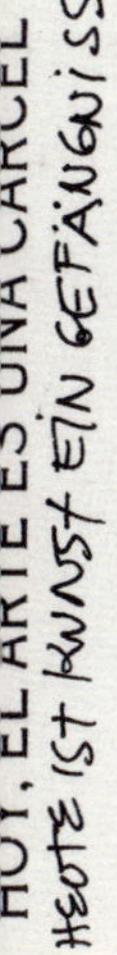

Horacio Zabala, Today Art is a Prision, mail art to Robert Rehfeldt via Galerie Arkade, 1978, paper, felt-tip pen, letterpress, 9.9 × 15 cm, Kupferstich-Kabinett, Staatliche Kunstsammlungen Dresden, inv. no. B 1979-15/196a

Clemente Padin, mail art to Ruth Wolf-Rehfeldt, 1976, paper, stamps, 34 × 22 cm, Mail Art Archive of Ruth Wolf-Rehfeldt and Robert Rehfeldt

alarming variant, that he is in prison precisely because he is an artist. All the possible readings allude to the frequent and unjust incarcerations of civilians suspected of dissidence, oftentimes artists, for those living in military dictatorships in Latin America between the 1960s to the 1980s.

The iconography of prison bars along with the theme of imprisonment were recurrent in mail art at this time, as manifested in a series of six postcards send by the Argentinean artist Horacio Zabala (b. 1943) to Rehfeldt via the Galerie Arkade. The postcards dated 1/IV/78 to 6/IV/78 each declare the same definitive phrase: "Hoy el arte es una carcel" (Today Art is a Prison) followed by the German "Heute ist Kunst ein Gefängniss [sic]". The theme was particularly valent following the highly publicized account of the imprisonment in 1977 of Uruguayan artists Clemente Padín (b. 1939) and Jorge Caraballo (b. 1941), both notorious figures in the mail art circuit.[9] Padín was jailed for distributing stamps in which he critiqued the military regime of Uruguay from 1973–1984 for their many human rights abuses much like the one he sent to the Rehfeldts in 1976 in which an anonymous, imprisoned figure is repeatedly duplicated in the medium of postal stamps. This work foreshadowed the artist's own future incarceration, as just a year later Padín was condemned to four years of prison during which he was prohibited from creating art or using the postal system. This injustice sparked an international outcry and mail artists mobilized on Padín and Caraballo's behalf pleading for their immediate release. Robert Rehfeldt, for example, sent a card that featured a photocopied image of Rembrandt behind bars headlined by the words "Freedom for Artists". The persistent volume of replies from artists all over the world appears to have had a direct effect on the situation by putting international pressure on the government and Padín was paroled in 1979, confined instead to home arrest.[10] Nevertheless, there were

9   The artists were convicted in a military court which applied Article 58, section II, of the Uruguayan military code for attacking the morale and reputation of the army. See Geoffrey Cook: The Padín/Caraballo Project, in: Correspondence Art. Source Book for Network of International Postal Art Activity, San Francisco 1984, p. 369–73. Reprinted: https://artpool.hu/MailArt/chrono/1984/Cook.html. (accessed on: 21.4.2023).

10   The mail art responses rallying for the artists' freedom were channeled through different forums, including official publications. For example, *DOC(K)S*, a popular magazine for visual poetry including mail art, edited by the French artist Julien Blaine, devoted a special issue to the Free Padín and Caraballo cause. The front cover of the April 1st, 1978 issue features a number of artists mail artworks showing support for the artists, including Robert Rehfeldt's piece mentioned here and Leonhard Duch's "Buracoarte" discussed later in this essay.

Robert Rehfeldt, Freedom for Artists/C. Padin/J. Caraballo, Uruguay, 1978, paper, letterpress, stamp print, 10.5 × 14.6 cm, Kupferstich-Kabinett, Staatliche Kunstsammlungen Dresden, inv. no. B 1979-15/17

Guillermo Deisler, 2500 Missing People, 1970s, postcard, screen print, 15.6 × 10.1 cm, Kupferstich-Kabinett, Staatliche Kunstsammlungen Dresden, inv. no. B 1979-15/75

lasting repercussions as Padín's valuable archive of mail art was seized and likely destroyed never to be found again. Despite the restrictions on his participation, Padín continued to be active member of the mail art network and just a few years after his house arrest he traveled to West-Berlin with the support of a DAAD grant (Deutscher Akademischer Austauschdienst), where he curated the exhibition *Mailart aus Lateinamerika* in 1984 at the DAAD Gallery in West-Berlin, including artists such as the Chilean Guillermo Deisler (1940–1995) and Duch mentioned earlier, among many others.[11] The exhibit brought greater notoriety to the mail art network's presence in Germany and to figures such as Deisler, living in exile in after escaping Chile in 1974.

Deisler is a notable figure in the dialogue between Latin America and the GDR where he lived and had connections to artists and other Chileans who like him were living there in exile.[12] Deisler was a vocal critic of Chile's repression and produced several series of postcards during the 1970s denouncing the Pinochet regime, as well as other military regimes in Latin America. During the 1980s, while in East Germany, Deisler lived and collaborated with Karla Sachse (b. 1950) and Joseph W. Huber (1951–2002), important figures in the GDR mail art network. After moving to Halle in 1986, Deisler began regularly publishing a collaborative portfolio of international mail art and visual poetry called *UNI/vers(;)*, which lasted from 1987 until his death in 1995. The process for producing this project was unique in that Deisler would send out a call for participation by mail and ask artists to send him their work in 100 "original" copies stamped with their signature. He then compiled the copies for the entire 100-copy print run of each issue, including his own work in each, which he then mailed to the participants and other collectors. The resulting 35 volumes are a testament to the graphic creativity exercised by the global community of artists at this time.[13]

Despite the relative freedom to correspond with artists internationally via the postal system, it is clear in retrospect that the mail and the postal system were under surveillance in Latin America and elsewhere. For example, the GDR graphic and mail artist, Jürgen Gottschalk (b. 1951) in Dresden was not only monitored but later imprisoned for two years

---

11   See for sample pages from the exhibition catalogue: https://artpool.hu/MailArt/chrono/1984/LatinAmerika.html (accessed on: 21.4.2023).

12   For example, artists such as Hernando Léon, a Professor at the Dresden Academy of Fine Arts and César Olhagaray who was granted asylum by the GDR in 1974 and was Léon's student.

13   For digital access to the volumes see https://monoskop.org/Univers (accessed on: 21.4.2023).

in 1984 before getting expatriated.[14] Nevertheless, artists continued to participate in the network, approaching the task of communicating subversive information in conceptually nuanced ways that permitted the exchange to continue and even flourish. One example demonstrating such graphic subtlety is Duch's 1978 project *Buracoarte* (Hole Art), in which he sent all the artists from his network, which numbered roughly three hundred artists, a postcard with a big black hole in the middle. On the addressee side, Duch instructed the artists in different languages to "put anything in the hole urgently and return to me ok?" He then compiled the returned postcards in a public exhibit at the *Second Winter Festival* at UNICAP (Catholic University of Pernambuco) in 1979 and later in a self-published, xeroxed version of the works which he sent to all those who participated. In Duch's own contribution to *Hole Art*, he included an image of himself behind bars within the hole of the postcard, a comment on the bleak circumstances surrounding him under the Brazilian dictatorship. This is reinforced by fellow Brazilian artist, J. Medeiros, who for his postcard inserted a torn-out section of a newspaper article about the information service, DOPS (The Department of Political and Social Order), notorious for inventive torture techniques.[15] In the torn-out newspaper article, the words "DOPS" alongside the fragment "delivered the bodies of subversive people" is enough to sound the alarm in the popular imagination, and despite not having access to the full article, the message is very clear.

The political ramifications of sending hundreds of people an image of a black hole from Brazil is symbolically charged, recasting Brazil as a site of trauma and alluding to the desperation surrounding the heightened violence of the dictatorship. What is particularly unique about Duch's project is that he did not just send out the missive but asked all the recipients to respond to it in whatever way they choose, albeit in the circumcised space of the hole. Robert Rehfeldt, for example, sent back a postcard from the GDR, with the handwritten "LOCHKUNST" (Hole Art) and "Vernichten" (Destroy) stamped onto the card. Inside the hole, Rehfeldt duplicates other holes in different sizes that look alarmingly like bullet holes, contained by a round stamp that reads "Postal Arte Creativa". A postcard from West Germany's Angelika Schmidt is more optimistic, featuring a handshake emerging out of the hole, a motif of solidarity and possibly reconciliation. By facilitating such visual encounters, Duch and mail artists more generally, instigated a forum for exchanging communication among distinct members of the international arts community by taking advantage of the global reach of the post office, despite the many existing political, economic, and social barriers in place.

Buracoarte [Hole Art], 1978, postcards by **Leonhard Frank Duch** (top), and **J. Medeiros** (bottom), 1978

14   For more information see the conference proceedings: Cordelia Marten: Conceptual Art in East Germany—Robert Rehfeldt and his network of artists, 2007, available at https://www.wkv-stuttgart.de/uploads/media/marten_en.pdf (accessed on: 21.4.2023) and Stefanie Schwabe: International Contact with Mail Art in the Spirit of Peaceful Coexistence. Birger Jesch's Mail Art Project (1980–81), in: Art beyond Borders: Artistic Exchange in Communist Europe (1945–1989), eds. Jérôme Bazin, Pascal Dubourg Glatigny, Piotr Piotrowski, Budapest, New York 2016, p. 255–63.

15   The Department of Political and Social Order was the secret police organ of the Brazilian government.

Buracoarte [Hole Art], postcards by **Robert Rehfeldt** (top), and **Angelika Schmidt** (bottom), 1978

Such encounters, particularly those between the GDR and Brazil and the rest of Latin America, became more prominent after Brazil's official recognition of the GDR in 1973, prompting a greater presence of art from the GDR in the *São Paulo Biennale*, a premier platform of visibility for artists from Europe in Latin America.[16] Prior to this, Brazil was reluctant to officially recognize a communist country, particularly as the dominant mission of the military was to violently root out any traces of communism in society. However, ultimately it was decided that the financial opportunities of reaching the Eastern Europe market via the GDR made it worthwhile. In 1977, the GDR was formally invited to participate in the *São Paulo Biennale* with only two works. A few years later, the *16th São Paulo Biennale* in 1981 featured five GDR artists. For this iteration, the curator Walter Zanini did away with national representation and instead organized the artworks through specially themed spaces, creating a large area for mail art. Over 500 artists sent in their work, among them artists discussed in this essay including Duch and Deisler, and from the GDR, Ruth and Robert Rehfeldt, Joseph W. Huber and Rolf Staeck (b. 1943).[17] Staeck's postcard was unequivocal in its criticism, featuring a head severed by a cradle knife hovering over a group of soldiers from which blood seems to drip down and form a halo around the troops.[18] The text in the middle is a quotation from the poem *Walking Around* (1933) by the Chilean poet Pablo Neruda in which the poet communicates the conflict between the individual and society, and more generally an emotion of hopelessness. In contrast the piece by Robert Rehfeldt was less overtly censorious, featuring a collage of texts which included an image of Josef Beuys, an important influence for him.[19] Rehfeldt stamped much of his mail art correspondence with "CONTART", a contraction of "Contact" and "Art" that became a defacto label for his work.

The activity of the mail art network slowed down significantly during the 1990s after the fall of the Berlin Wall and artists like Duch no longer felt the political urgency to communicate across the East/West divide. Ruth Wolf-Rehfeldt deliberately stopped making art at all in 1991, while other artists who were very active in the network expanded their graphic repertoire and to this day work with a diversity of media. Nevertheless, the textual and visual missives that comprise the individual and institutional mail art archives provide for a fascinating way to glimpse and rethink the possibilities and stakes of artistic exchange and communication. Mail artworks continue to inspire examination and they perform an archival function, acting as documents and traces of encounters enacted in a context that

16   See the front-page announcement of the official recognition in *Estado de São Paulo*, a major newspaper on October 23, 1973.

17   Staeck was accused of cultural underground activity in 1983 and shortly after moved to Heidelberg in West Germany, where his brother, the well-known poster artist Klaus Staeck, lived.

18   To see Staeck's and other artist contributions to the mail art section, see the online exhibition catalogue for *16ª Bienal de São Paulo (1981) – Exposição Arte Postal*: https://issuu.com/bienal/docs/name4dc6c4/119 (accessed on: 21.4.2023).

19   Ibid.

did its best to deter such a dialogue. I want to close by acknowledging that my own encounter of the intercontinental mailed works led me to navigate all manner of different mail art collections, all diverse in their holdings and configuration. While there is no centralized archive of mail art, many of the artists working in this mode were meticulous cataloguers committed to the value of these poetic, aesthetic and sometimes subversive global, postal missives that traveled and circulated across borders against the odds and continue to inspire further examination.[20]

20   While the existing archives of mail art are entirely decentralized, often existing with the artists themselves, a few online examples stand out for their substantial holdings. See https://www.lomholtmailartarchive.dk/; https://artpool.hu/institute/about.html; https://mailartists.wordpress.com/; https://mailartists.wordpress.com/ (accessed on: 21.4.2023).

Hector Tobar, The Honourable Junta, sheet 4 from the series *On the History of the Communist Party of Chile*, 1975, woodcut, 79.8 × 58.8 cm, Kunstfonds, Staatliche Kunstsammlungen Dresden, inv. no. 1d/1/76

Guillermo Deisler, Big Business for the Yankees, 1970s, postcard, screen print, 9.6 × 11.4 cm, Kupferstich-Kabinett, Staatliche Kunstsammlungen Dresden, inv. no. B 1979-15/76

Gerhard Bondzin, The Invincibles, 1967, mixed media on canvas, 157 × 215 cm, Albertinum, Staatliche Kunstsammlungen Dresden, Gal. no. 3686

U Sein Linn, Untitled, from a series of 10 prints on the liberation struggle against the Japanese occupation force in Burma (1942–1945), 1978, lithograph, 50 × 37.5 cm, Kustodie der Hochschule für Bildende Künste Dresden, inv. no. B 2330

U Sein Linn studied 1973–1975 at the Academy of Fine Arts in Dresden.

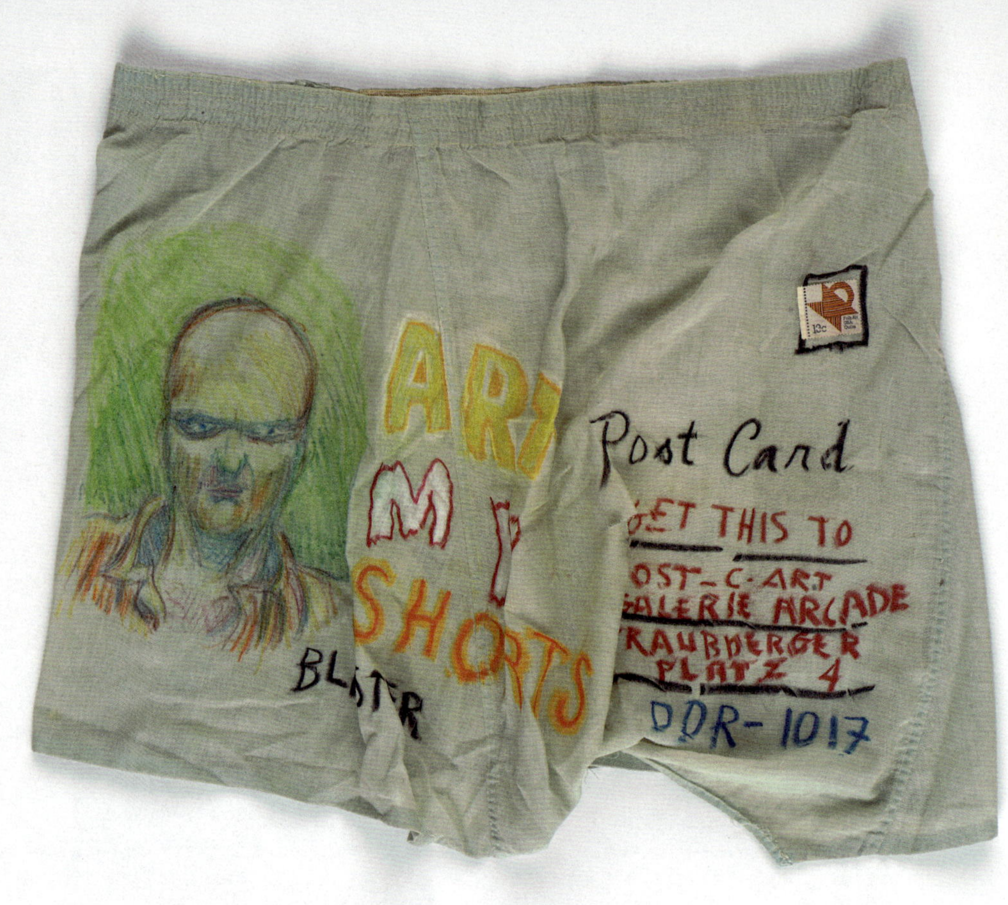

Blaster Al Ackermann, Art My Shorts, 1978, mixed fabric, stamp, color pencils, c. 42 × 48 cm, Kupferstich-Kabinett, Staatliche Kunstsammlungen Dresden, inv. no. B 1979-15/24

60

The special thing about mail art is that it is non-commercial, that it is open to anyone who wants to take part and draws no boundaries. And that it also tries to overcome borders internationally. Borders of language, of cultures, national borders, political ones. Freedom was the most important thing for us.

The artist Lutz Wohlrab on the significance of mail art in the GDR, interview as part of the research project *Art in Networks—The GDR and its Global Relations*, see p. 171.

Andrei Mylnikov, The Awakening of Africa (For Peace and Independence), 1957, oil on canvas, 300 × 280 cm, State Russian Museum, St. Petersburg, PM RCP6R9

Petra Lange-Berndt

Studio H&S in the Global Nexus: Documentary Films about the Congo in the German Democratic Republic, 1965/66

From 1960 onwards, a number of former European colonies in sub-Saharan Africa, such as Cameroon, Togo, the Congo, the Republic of Dahomey (now Benin) and Nigeria, obtained independence. There was hope that the former world order had come to an end; Pan-Africanism and the Organisation of African Unity were talking points. Simultaneously, the region had been engaging since the end of the Second World War in more interchange with the Soviet Union. Official Communist policy defined Western imperialism as a product of capitalist structures and was seeking to forge new political alliances: in Moscow, the Peoples' Friendship University of Russia opened in 1960, facilitating exchange with students from Africa.[1] It was in this context, in 1957, that the artist Andrei Andreyevich Mylnikov created his monumental oil painting *The Awakening of Africa: For Peace and Independence*, a declaration of solidarity where confident Black protagonists hold the center stage.[2] The group, dressed in traditional clothes, strides towards us amid a cheering throng and are welcomed by representatives of the Arab and Latin American communities and of the Soviet empire.[3] This foreign policy was not solely about supporting a just cause, socialism and communism were globalising too: Amid the wave of decolonisation, the superpowers were vying for influence in this part of the world.[4]

Mass media like photography, film and television played a central role in this context. Several Soviet protagonists, for example, set out on journeys to generate footage for news reports and documentaries, not least *We Are with You, Africa* (dir.: Danilov L., USSR, 1963).[5] At around this time, the East German journalist Walter Heynowski (b. 1927) also resolved to tackle the topic. In the course of his work for GDR television, he had produced contributions in the style of documentary filmmaker Andrew Thorndike, using audiovisual material as if it were evidence laid before a court.[6] The 35-minute, black-and-white short film *Kommando 52*, on which I shall focus here, was delivered by Heynowski to DEFA's documentary arm, the Studio für Wochenschau und Dokumentarfilme, in 1965. He had made it together with the West German cameraman Peter Hellmich, who had been working for DEFA from the West since 1953. The editor was Traute Wischnewski.[7]

Kommando 52 is a pivotal work in many ways. It marks the formation of Studio H&S, a collective with close government ties that consisted not only of Heynowski, Hellmich and Wischnewski but also journalist Gerhard Scheumann (1930–1998). Its members enjoyed a unique special status and numerous privileges. Until 1982 they served the global class struggle on various Cold War fronts. From 1 May 1969, Studio H&S operated independently

1   For general background see Christian Saehrendt: Kunst im Kampf für das „Sozialistische Weltsystem". Auswärtige Kulturpolitik der DDR in Afrika und Nahost, Stuttgart 2017.
2   W.B. Blek: Der Monumentalmaler und Lyriker Andrej Mylnikow, in: Bildende Kunst, 1960, no. 4, p. 241–245, here p. 245.
3   Ibid., p. 242.
4   See Mark Nash: Things Fall Apart, in: Red Africa: Affective Communities and the Cold War, ed. Mark Nash, London 2016, p. 6–19; Immanuel R. Harisch, Eric Burton: Sozialistische Globalisierung. Tagebücher der DDR-Freundschaftsbrigaden in Afrika, Asien und Lateinamerika, in: Zeithistorische Forschungen/Studies in Contemporary History 17 (2020), no. 3, p. 578–591.
5   Alexander Markov, "Our Africa", in Nash 2016 (note 4), p. 44–47, here p. 44.
6   Rüdiger Steinmetz: Die Film- und Fernseh-Dokumentaristen Walter Heynowski und Gerhard Scheumann, in: Dokumentarfilm zwischen Beweis und Pamphlet. Heynowski & Scheumann und Gruppe Katins, eds. Rüdiger Steinmetz, Tilo Prase, Leipzig 2002, p. 13–158, here p. 31.
7   Gerhard Scheumann was only marginally involved in *Kommando 52*, see Steinmetz 2002 (note 6), p. 48. Peter Hellmich and Gerhard Scheumann were both confidential informants for the Ministry for State Security, see Christian Bunnenberg: Der „Kongo-Müller". Eine deutsche Söldnerkarriere, Berlin 2007, p. 87.

from DEFA but was in regular touch with the Foreign Ministry of the GDR, the foreign policy department of the SED's Central Committee and occasionally the foreign intelligence wing of the Ministry for State Security.[8] The team were well known for products devoted to (anti-)colonialist and liberation struggles in the Global South, including Vietnam and Chile. *Kommando 52* does not address the ideal of peaceful, transnational concord of the kind stylised by Mylnikov in his painting. Instead, the film is a dramatic account of the 'Congo Crisis', an extremely bloody and complex conflict that was unfolding at that time. In 1960, upon achieving independence, the country had elected Patrice Lumumba as the first prime minister of its postcolonial state. However, under pressure from the United States and the former colonial power Belgium (there were economic interests at stake), he was removed from his post by the country's first president, Joseph Kasa-Vubu. Lumumba was eventually assassinated by an execution squad in the presence of Belgian officers and officials and the events that followed verged on civil war. The Mouvement National Congolais, which had close ties with Lumumba and socialist sympathies, was fighting against an alliance led by prime minister Moïse Tschombé. What particularly interested Heynowski and Hellmich about this scenario was that, once the United Nations peacekeeping force made up of African troops left the Congo, Tschombé was supported not only by the army under chief-of-staff Joseph-Désiré Mobutu but also by the West, including *white* mercenaries endorsed by the United States and Belgium. Among them were West German men who signed up for armed units like the mercenary '52 Commando'. In November 1965, the dictator Mobuto finally declared himself president with the help of Western intelligence services and disbanded the mercenary units.[9]

These conflicts during the Cold War amounted to a brutal proxy war between the superpowers of the day, and *Kommando 52* is a work with a clear political position. The film was highly successful in the GDR and won the 'Goldene Taube', the top prize at the Leipzig Documentary Film Festival, where it was screened on 16 November 1965.[10] In West Germany, meanwhile, it was officially banned as propaganda and placed on the list of restricted works.[11] Productions at Studio H&S were based, especially in the 1970s, on trips to the countries concerned and interaction with the participants. In the mid-1960s, just after the Berlin Wall went up and at a time when the GDR was fighting for international recognition as a sovereign state by countries outside the Eastern bloc, visiting the Congo to make *Kommando 52* was out of the question. Walter Heynowski and Peter Hellmich had to come up with a work-around. In the film itself and in the press, the duo claimed that the documents they had drawn on had been obtained by Congolese patriots and posted to West Germany, where they were intercepted and passed on to Hellmich.[12] That was not, however, the truth of the matter. In fact, the filmmakers had gone on a fishing expedition among West German media.[13] From September 1964 onwards, reports on German mercenaries in the Congo had been appearing in the weekly magazines *Quick* and *Revue*, illustrated with images taken in the Congo by West German journalists.[14] These stories carried black-

---

8   For general background see Robert Michel: Die Filme Heynowski & Scheumann, Peter Hellmich 1965–1978. deutsch, english, français, español, ed. Robert Michel, Berlin 1979; Studio H&S: Walter Heynowski und Gerhard Scheumann. Filme 1964–1989, box with 5 DVDs and accompanying booklet, ed. Ralf Schenk, absolut MEDIEN GmbH, TELEPOOL GmbH, Defa-Stiftung, 2014; Steinmetz 2002 (note 6), p. 61–66; Günter Jordan, Ralf Schenk, eds., Schwarzweiß und Farbe. DEFA-Dokumentarfilme 1946–92, Berlin 1996.

9   Matthias Steinle: Vom Feindbild zum Fremdbild. Die gegenseitige Darstellung von BRD und DDR im Dokumentarfilm, Konstanz 2003, p. 295; Bunnenberg 2007 (note 7), p. 40–46, 58.

10   The film ran at cinemas from 10 December 1965; Bunnenberg 2007 (note 7), p. 88.

11   Ibid., p. 89.

12   Ibid.

13   Ibid., p. 80.

14   Karl Breyer (photographs), Peter Leukefeld (text): Das letzte Aufgebot, in: Quick, no. 38, September 20, 1964, p. 40–46 (with additional images by the French photographer Yves-Guy Bergès); anonymous: Tränen um den toten Sohn, in: Quick, no. 39, September 27, 1964, p. 134; Siegfried Müller: Ich, Hauptmann Müller, in: Revue, no. 41, October 11, 1964, p. 22–25, 94; Elfriede Müller: Mein Mann, der Hauptmann, in: Revue, no. 42, October 18, 1964, p. 90–93; Herbert Kaufhold: Flieh, Kaffer oder stirb, in: Revue, no. 43, October 25, 1964, p. 34–38.

and-white photographs, sometimes full-page, which, despite the context of their publication in the sensational press, are marked as authentic by their coarse grain and the accompanying text. From today's standpoint it is shocking to see corpses displayed right next to adverts like the one for razor blades of the brand Rotbart Rostfrei "for many silky shaves"—it is hard to imagine a more cynical montage.[15] Overall, the coverage echoes the perspective of the European and above all German mercenaries and their relatives back home in West Germany. In the words of historian Christian Bunnenberg, it reeks of "belated German Africa Corps despatches from the front".[16] The articles are uncritical and racist; they are also biased in only presenting the angle of the former colonial powers, their supporters and Moïse Tschombé. The latter was received as a guest in West Germany during that period; evidently the Federal German government had no reservations about *white* hegemony, for it was also an ally of the apartheid regime in South Africa. And the observation that there were former members of the SS among the mercenaries did not strike *Quick*, for example, as worthy of any further comment at a time when former Nazi bigwigs still held public office.[17] This media attention eventually culminated in late 1964 in four reports in the illustrated magazine *Stern* produced by journalist Ernst Petry and photographer Gerd Heidemann during a trip to the Congo and a visit to the mercenary '52 Commando'.[18] While there are signs of racism here too, the perspective this time is different, as the journalists do express criticism of Tschombé and West European involvement in the conflict. The reports make it clear that there have been violations of human rights: murders, pillaging, torture. And it is these reports in *Stern* that form the basis for the film *Kommando 52*. After Peter Hellmich's attention was caught by the material, he went with Heynowski to visit the reporter Gerd Heidemann in Hamburg, from whom the duo purchased images, letters and copies of tape recordings.[19] The "Congolese patriots" turned out in retrospect to have been West German journalists and the postal piracy was a case of secondary publication.

This material was then edited into a film, creating the impression that the filmmakers had been right there on the spot. The first thing seen by the audience is a photograph in a developing tray, where an image depicting the corpse of a Black person slowly appears, signalling the evidential quality of the photograph. The red light of the dark room brooks no shades of grey, no nuances, only a harsh contrast between black and white. The rhythm of the story with its omniscient narrator, spoken by actor Herwart Grosse, is relentless as we are confronted with such diverse sources as original sound from the mercenaries, stills, letters, diaries and 16-mm footage.[20] The spoken commentary is laconic and the focus is on the images, which trigger powerful emotional reactions; the film was licensed for viewers over 18.[21] We see corpses, corpses, nothing but corpses, in close-up, tortured, mutilated, half rotting. *Kommando 52* documents the killings and the inappropriate conduct of the mercenaries in detail, describing extreme forms of cruelty and inhuman atrocities applied even to dead bodies. The point is emphatically made that mercenaries in the Congo shoot people twice: with guns and, like ordinary tourists, with cameras (implicitly, that likewise

15 Kaufhold 1964 (note 14), p. 34–35.
16 Bunnenberg 2007 (note 7), p. 78.
17 Breyer, Leukefeld 1964 (note 14), p. 46.
18 Ernst Petry, Gerd Heidemann: Auf der Straße der Landsknechte, in: Stern, no. 47, November 22, 1964, p. 40–50; Ernst Petry: Die Straße der Landsknechte (2), in: Stern, no. 48, November 29, 1964, p. 93–99; Ernst Petry: Auf der Straße der Landsknechte (3), in: Stern, no. 49, December 6, 1964, p. 112–118; Ernst Petry: Unser Vater blieb im Kongo, in: Stern, no. 50, December 13, 1964, p. 12–19, 123–131. Journalist Dieter Heggemann was also on the team but did not take part in these expeditions, see Bunnenberg 2007 (note 7), p. 11–12. Gerd Heidemann would raise eyebrows again in April 1983 in connection with the publication of faked Hitler diaries in Stern.
19 See Bunnenberg 2007 (note 7), p. 88–91; Walter Heynowski and Gerd Heidemann claim that Stern's publisher Henri Nannen knew about the venture—on this see the television report Kongo Müller. Eine deutsch-deutsche Geschichte, written and directed by Siegfried Ressel (ZDF) in collaboration with arte, 2011.
20 For an overview see Bunnenberg 2007 (note 7), p. 88–92; on Grosse see https://www.defa-stiftung.de/filme/filme-suchen/kommando-52/ (accessed on: 28.4.2023).
21 Steinmetz 2002 (note 6), p. 34; Bunnenberg 2007 (note 7), p. 88.

Kommando 52, director: Walter Heynowski, documentary, b/w, 34 min, GDR, DEFA-Studio für Wochenschau und Dokumentarfilme, 1965 (film stills)

applies to the West German photographers).[22] In this sense, *Kommando 52* served as a cinematographic weapon, as "(visual) counterfire" with which the GDR was actively supporting the struggle of the socialist liberation movement.[23] The film made no claim to be neutral in reporting on events in the Congo. Instead, the protagonists used the documentary material to assemble an alternative, in the spirit of socialist realism, to the presentations in the Western gutter press, as Studio H&S stated programmatically in 1980: "The workshop professes its ideology openly and in every public arena [...]. It adopts a decisive polemic against the position of a detached, impartial objectivism that is exposed again and again for its dissembling and its dishonourable agenda."[24] In this manner, with reference to the practice of the filmmaker Dziga Vertov[25] and drawing heavily in the last third on Sergei Eisenstein's montage of attractions—contrasts and parallels, shot and countershot— the film formulates clear charges, underpinning them with evidence as if before a court: the Federal Republic of Germany is an active neocolonialist force and West German authorities in the Church, politics and industry are backing the Tschombé regime and fuelling events in the Congo.[26] Moreover, a direct correlation is established between the presence of German mercenaries in the Congo and the deployment of the United States Army in Vietnam. A sequence from a Nazi education film made in summer 1944 demonstrates that German fascism is still alive, and at the end the audience can hear the murderers confessing over an evening camp fire as music by Beethoven fades in under the text: "We as Germans are ashamed of the German crimes revealed by this film."

Kommando 52 hit a nerve. Accompanied by an extensive press campaign in the GDR, Studio H&S made more films on similar topics: *Der lachende Mann* (1966), *PS zum lachenden Mann* (1966) and *Der Fall Bernd K.* (1967). Three books were published alongside the films, including *Kannibalen* (1967), and the long-playing record *Der lachende Mann – Bekenntnisse eines Mörders* (1966).[27] The *Congo Triptych* painted by Heinz Lohmar in 1965 can also be placed in this context (p. 94/95). Before the première of *Kommando 52*, Studio H&S were already planning their documentary *Der lachende Mann*, which was broadcast on East German television by Deutscher Fernsehfunk on 9 February 1966 and released in cinemas

22 See also Heynowski & Scheumann: Kannibalen. Ein abendländisches Poesiealbum in Selbstzeugnissen, Berlin 1967, p. 24.

23 Steinle 2003 (note 9), p. 296.

24 Robert Michel: Kurzfilmwerkstatt Studio H&S. Materialien eines auswärtigen Seminars, in: Filmwissenschaftliche Beiträge 21 (1980), no.2, p. 7–32, here p. 12; Dokumentarfilm, Dokumentarisches, in: Kulturpolitisches Wörterbuch, eds. Manfred Berger et al., Berlin 1978, p. 144–146.

25 See the report about the seminar on political documentary film held during the retrospective at Den Danske Filmskole in Copenhagen on 16 and 17 April 1977, in: H&S im Gespräch. Mit Filmen im Ausland. Eine Dokumentation, ed. Robert Michel (= Information 1977, no. 4, published by the Hochschule für Film und Fernsehen der DDR), p. 4–26, here p. 4.

26 Steinle 2003 (note 9), p. 294–299; Bunnenberg 2007 (note 7), p. 15–16, 88–89.

27 Other books associated with the films were Der lachende Mann (1966, two editions) and Der Fall Bernd K. (1968)—see Bunnenberg 2007 (note 7), p. 86, 93–94.

on 18 March. With this work the collective finally wrote media history,[28] because they managed to interview the commander of the mercenary 52 Commando, Major Siegfried Müller aka 'Congo-Müller', dressed in military uniform complete with his Iron Cross 1st Class adorned by a swastika, on 10 November 1965 in Munich. The former mercenary agreed to the interview in the belief that he was talking to West German journalists. The interview was conducted by Gerhard Scheumann, who worked as an editor and presenter for the TV magazine *Prisma* from 1963 until 1965 and had established a reputation there as an investigative journalist who did not flinch from criticising the GDR. This constellation was as ideal as it was unique. The class enemy sat under a spotlight in a black-lined room, where the audience could study him carefully. In the course of the conversation, the guest with the symbolically charged name revealed himself more and more blatantly to be a chilling proponent of (neo-)fascism and living proof of neocolonialism in West Germany.[29] Here and there Studio H&S interspersed the recorded interview with documentary footage from *Kommando 52*— not least to refute Müller's claims. The film was a huge success and was exported to 37 Eastern Bloc countries and non-aligned states.[30] Together with *Kommando 52* it contrasts sharply with films like *Africa Addio* (Africa Blood and Guts), which was made in 1966. The 132-minute documentary by Gualtiero Jacopetti and Franco Prosperi likewise addressed decolonisation in Africa and included images from the Congo. The Italian directors, however, presented the conflict as a result of the withdrawal of European colonial powers. Most significantly of all, for entertainment value Jacopetti and Prosperi had filmed an attack carried out by the mercenaries of 52 Commando on 24 October 1964.[31] While *Der lachende Mann* was placed on the index of films banned in West Germany,[32] the racist jaw-dropper *Africa Addio* not only survived cinematic self-censorship but even, as the West German journalist Otto Köhler sarcastically commented, was awarded "the tax-saving rating 'recommended'".[33] This prompted students, some of them Black, to stage a solidarity protest in West Berlin against an official visit to West Germany by Moïse Tschombé and against *Africa Addio*, as *PS zum lachenden Mann* records.

Kommando 52, director: Walter Heynowski, documentary, b/w, 34 min, GDR, DEFA-Studio für Wochenschau und Dokumentarfilme, 1965 (film stills)

28 For an overview of *Der lachende Mann* see Steinmetz 2002 (note 6), p. 72–87; Bunnenberg 2007 (note 7), p. 95–100.
29 Siegfried evokes a Germanic hero abused by Nazi-ideology while the very common surname Müller might stand for the West German population in general.
30 Bunnenberg 2007 (note 7), p. 100.
31 Ibid., p. 56–57.
32 Steinle 2003 (note 9), p. 299.
33 Otto Köhler: Kongo-Müller oder Die Freiheit, die wir verteidigen. Mit einem Stenogramm von Alexander Mitscherlich, Frankfurt am Main 1966, p. 68–69.

Kommando 52 and the subsequent films enabled the GDR to present itself, in line with Soviet globalisation policy at the time, as the Congo's champion. This advocacy was not confined to films. Since February 1966, the 'workers' and farmers' state' had been attracting media headlines with a campaign for Müller to be indicted under criminal law. At a press conference held by the East German delegation on 16 February 1966 during the International Short Film Festival in Oberhausen, trial by cinema finally gave way to trial by court. *Kommando 52* and *Der lachende Mann* were not screened. Instead, the renowned East Berlin lawyer Friedrich Karl Kaul, counsel to Studio H&S, issued a press statement to the effect that he had filed charges of murder on various counts and aggravated robbery against Siegfried Müller and his aide-de-camp Gerd von Blottnitz at the high court in Frankfurt am Main on behalf of "1. Pauline Lumumba", the wife of the assassinated prime minister, "2. Mr Gabriel Yumbu, 3. Mr Léon Lokongo, 4. Mr Camille Khumu, 5. Mr Michele Mougai, 6. Mr Placid Kutungwa".[34] Kaul was a well-considered choice as claimant. The high court in Berlin had licensed him to practice before the city's judicial systems were broken up by Germany's partition, and this meant that he could also join actions before

Congolese students from Leipzig's Karl Marx University look at the street sign of Lumumba Street, named after the first prime minister of Congo, Patrice Lumumba, on the occasion of the Week of Friendship and Solidarity of the Freie Deutsche Jugend (Free German Youth). Leipzig, 26.4.1961, photo: Heinz Koch

West German courts.[35] This status enabled him to take part from 1963 until 1965 in the first Auschwitz trial heard in Frankfurt. In this context, the "presentation of anti-Communist and racist statements by the mercenaries in conjunction with the images of Congolese citizens who had been tortured and murdered" raised the issue in both German states of a "new type of German war crime" in Africa.[36] Siegfried Müller, however, escaped to South Africa and never returned to West Germany. On 13 September 1966, *PS zum lachenden Mann* was premièred on GDR television.[37] The film shows, just one year after Walter Ulbricht was officially received by Egypt's president Gamal Abdel Nasser, a visit by Heynowski and Scheumann to Cairo, where they conducted an interview with Lumumba's widow Pauline, seeking and carrying out a direct exchange with a major protagonist from the Congo.[38]

The films by Studio H&S occupy an ambivalent position between information and propaganda.[39] In flagging up the colonial and postcolonial entanglements between the Federal Republic of Germany and Africa and the military deployments undertaken in that context, the East German documentaries with their partial but clearly marked perspective identify a problem that has still not been subjected to proper analysis. However, the partisan thrust of the films prevented a full exploration of the issue. The documentaries pursue the argument, for example, that it was above all West German mercenaries under the command of Siegfried

34   Ibid., p. 12–15; Bunnenberg 2007 (note 7), p. 106–107.

35   Annette Weinke: Die Verfolgung von NS-Tätern im geteilten Deutschland. Vergangenheitsbewältigung 1949–1969 oder: Eine deutsch-deutsche Beziehungsgeschichte im Kalten Krieg, Paderborn 2002, p. 253.

36   Bunnenberg 2007 (note 7), p. 90–91.

37   Claudia Böttcher, Judith Kretzschmar, Corinna Schier: Heynowski & Scheumann – Dokumentarfilmer im Klassenkampf. Eine kommentierte Filmographie, Leipzig 2002, p. 113.

38   I am grateful to Martina Seidel, Deutsches Rundfunkarchiv, for her assistance with this research.

39   Steinle 2003 (note 9), p. 292.

Müller who stood for the continuity of the Nazi regime and its crimes. And yet citizens of what was by now the GDR had also played their part in German fascism. Moreover, the filmmakers claimed that Müller was acting on orders from the Federal Republic, although the former Wehrmacht soldier, who attended US officer training after the war, had never served in the Bundeswehr. In the Congo he was working under former British officers for Tschombé.[40] And the mercenaries doing the killing in the Congo came not only from West Germany, but also from Britain, Belgium, Italy, France, Rhodesia and South Africa.[41] This ultimately begs the question what the precisely composed films on the Congo by Heynowski and Studio H&S do *not* tell us: for example, that left-wing organisations in the Federal Republic were articulating criticism of Germany's colonial history. Such debates had to be glossed over in silence, as did the racism that occurred in the 'workers' and farmers' state', in order to uphold the narrative of a neocolonial West Germany and an East Germany intent on solidarity with Africa.[42] Besides, at least one copy of *Der lachende Mann* had arrived in West Germany and was being screened by Helmut Soeder, an insurance salesman in Freiburg and peace movement activist, and by the Sozialistischer Deutscher Studentenbund, an association of socialist college students.[43] Apart from this, Otto Köhler published his book on the subject, *Kongo-Müller oder Die Freiheit, die wir verteidigen*, reproducing large chunks of Scheumann's interview with Müller—in the face of resistance from the GDR.[44] In the final analysis, *Kommando 52*, *Der lachende Mann* and *PS zum lachenden Mann* remain trapped

40   Bunnenberg 2007 (note 7), p. 20, 48.
41   Ibid., p. 13.
42   On the integration problems facing African college and school students and contract workers see Saehrendt 2017 (note 1), p. 43–44.
43   Ibid., p. 101.
44   Köhler 1966 (note 33), p. 19, 73; Bunnenberg 2007 (note 7), p. 103–104.

in the relationship between the two Germanies, a perspective that relegated the Congolese themselves to the passive status of victims. While the films do address the complex ways in which the domestic population were embroiled in the conflict, they gave them no voice— literally, for even Pauline Lumumba's words were dubbed by a female East German actor. *Kommando 52* in particular lends itself to the accusation that its engagement with politics is founded on extremely problematic recordings and that no attempt was made to involve families or survivors in a broader discussion about how to go about appropriate, ethically responsible reporting. The audiences are turned into accomplices, not only of West Germany's neocolonial aspirations, and we recognise that we are party to a voyeuristic media spectacle. On these grounds, and until there has been a thorough assessment in collaboration with stakeholders from the Democratic Republic of the Congo, *Kommando 52* should only be screened in academic research settings. That is the only way to counter this variety of globalisation with fitting critique.

Translated by: Kate Vanovitch

Jürgen Schieferdecker, How Africa Was Set Free, 1977, color letterpress on polyester film, mounted on newspaper page, 34.5 × 27.5 cm, Kunstfonds, Staatliche Kunstsammlungen Dresden, inv.-no. G 106/2000

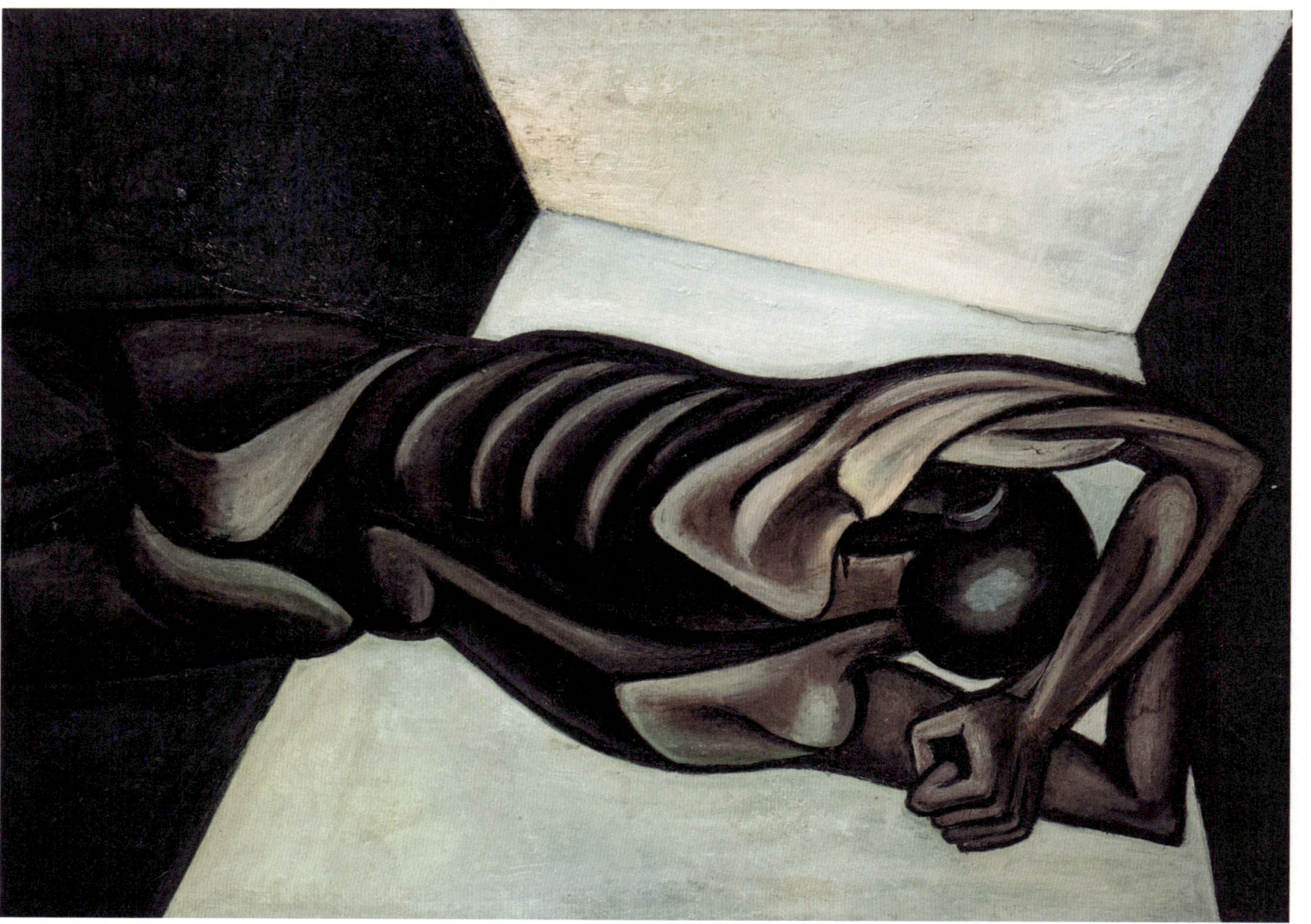

Afonso Lana Leite, Man and Walls, 1981, oil on canvas, 140 × 104.5 cm,
Kustodie der Hochschule für Bildende Künste Dresden, inv. no. A 0660
Afonso Lana Leite studied 1976–1981 at the Academy of Fine Arts in Dresden.

Daoud Slaman Anad, The Prophet, 1975, mixed media on canvas, 120 × 100 cm, Albertinum, Staatliche Kunstsammlungen Dresden, inv. no. 82/14

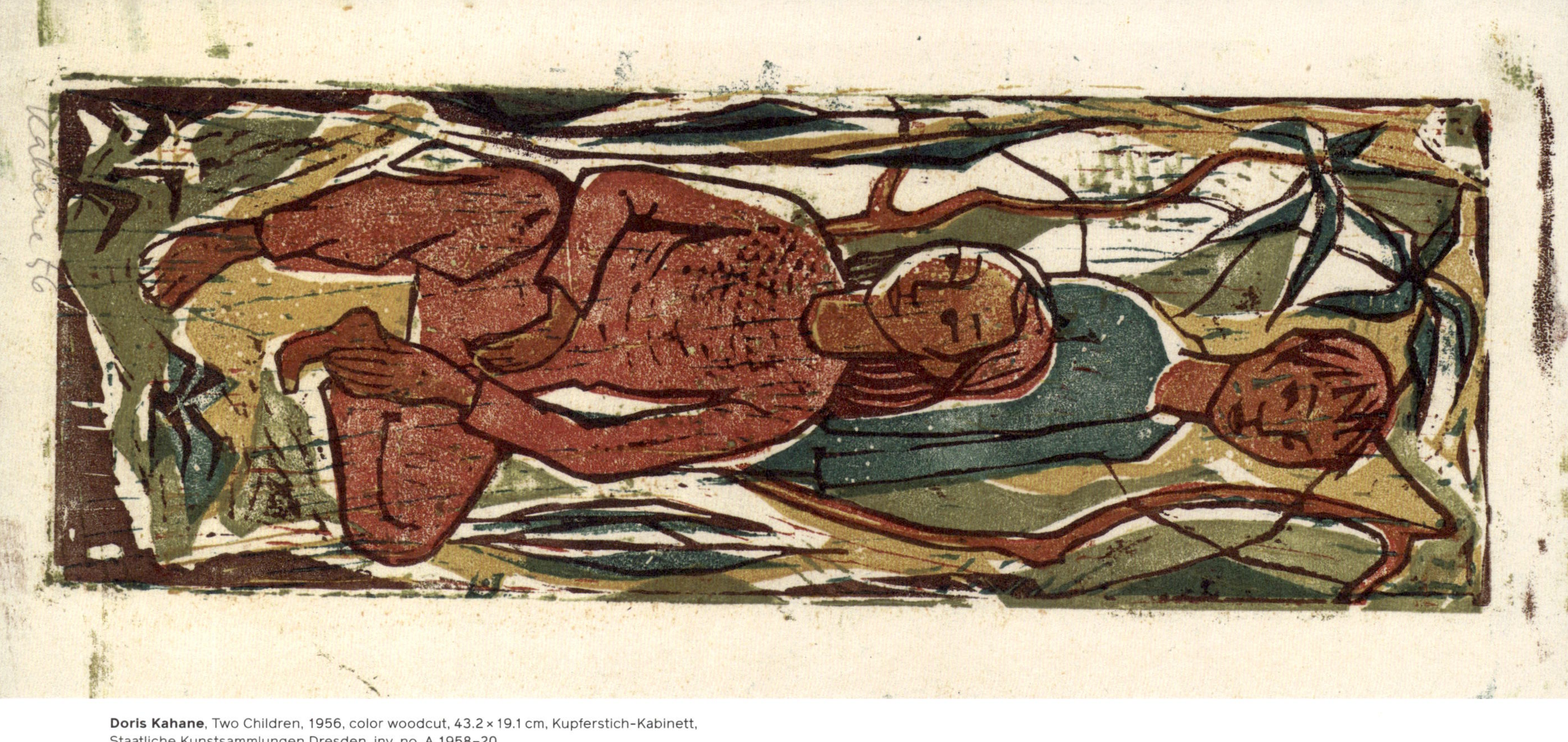

Doris Kahane, Two Children, 1956, color woodcut, 43.2 × 19.1 cm, Kupferstich-Kabinett,
Staatliche Kunstsammlungen Dresden, inv. no. A 1958–20

I was young and had this euphoria, this joy of being able to study at an art college in Europe. For someone from the Caribbean, it's a completely different world, of course; it's impressive and very, very special to be able to study in Europe. So, that is a privilege.

The artist Teresa Casanueva on her journey from Cuba to the GDR and her studies at Burg Giebichenstein in Halle (Saale) in the 1980s, interview as part of the research project *Art in Networks—The GDR and its Global Relations*, see p. 171.

Georges Adéagbo b. 1942

African Students and Socialism, 2023, installation, various objects and materials, dimensions variable

Albertinum, Staatliche Kunstsammlungen Dresden, on loan from the Gesellschaft für Moderne Kunst in Dresden e.V.

For several decades, Georges Adéagbo has pursued an artistic practice based on collecting and combining heterogeneous objects. The artist's complex composite installations consist of used and new things, antiques and mass-produced goods, found objects and commissioned works. Books, sculptures, paintings, records, clothing, newspaper clippings, bric-a-brac-everything is worthy of entering Adéagbo's non-hierarchical and transcultural archive. A central characteristic of his working

method is the mobilization of things: He carries them from his home in Cotonou, Benin, to the exhibition venues, but also, conversely, takes things home with him to be used as models for paintings and sculptures, which he commissions from local artisans and integrates into new installations. On the one hand, the themes of exhibitions are developed in his studio in Cotonou, where he writes texts and sets up ephemeral installations on a daily basis. On the other hand, he expands these themes by adding objects from the future exhibition site. Hence, all objects are connected to the respective specific place as if in a network of associations, but they are also linked to other places, opening up a field of tension between 'global' and 'local' references. This variant of site-specific work could be called 'relational site-specificity'.

For the exhibition *Revolutionary Romances?* Adéagbo, in collaboration with his long-time curator Stephan Köhler, explored the GDR's relations with socialist brother countries in Africa. Adéagbo selected artworks from collections in Dresden and had them repainted in Cotonou by local painter Benoît Adanhoumé, who signs his works with the artist's name 'Esprit Petit Frère'. Adéagbo's interest was primarily sparked by portraits of students from Africa, for example, that of Chukwuemeka Ogbue, who had come from Nigeria to study in the GDR and was portrayed by Eva Schulze-Knabe in 1960 in a reading pose (p. 107). Having these paintings copied in the style of African sign painting can be understood as an appreciation of and, at the same time, a distancing from the motifs. In combination with short commentary texts by Adéagbo, this initiates a process of appropriation and translation.

Kerstin Schankweiler

Martin Angermann
around 1918–?

The Friendship of the Youth of
all Peace-Loving Peoples
Ensures Peace for the World,
1951, hanging chandelier
with five carved and painted
figures, 1951, wood,
18 × 49.5 cm

Museum für Sächsische Volkskunst,
Staatliche Kunstsammlungen Dresden,
inv. no. G 8523

The candelabra demonstrates how, in the
GDR, the ideologized ideas of international
friendship and peacekeeping were not only
themes in the visual arts but also found
expression in folk art and amateur artistic
creation. In 1951, East Berlin hosted the
Third World Festival of Youth and Students.
In his candelabra, created in the same year,
Angermann took up the motif of a global,
multicultural community of nations, which
was also propagated in the logo, posters
and postcards of the World Festival. Its
figures represent the five continents; in their
stereotypical portrayal, they reflect the
folkloristic classification of people from

different continents and cultures that
was prevalent at the time. This reflects the
imperial perspective of so-called 'Socialist
Chromatism': the uncritical, striking
illustration of the idea of international friendship based on supposed 'ethnographic'
archetypes, operating with cultural attributions and exoticisms. At the same time,
the candelabra represents an example of
how a traditional type of candle holder (that
is also associated with religious practices)
was transformed into a socialist object of
everyday use, with an ideological message
that Angermann carved into the wooden ring:
"The Friendship of the Youth of all Peace-
Loving Peoples Ensures Peace for the World".

Mathias Wagner

Walter Arnold
1909–1979

Forward and Never Forget—
Solidarity, 1967, wood,
93.5 × 60 × 31 cm

Kunstfonds, Staatliche Kunstsammlungen
Dresden, inv. no. 75/67

Walter Arnold was appointed head of the Department of Sculpture at the Dresden Academy of Fine Arts in 1951 and quickly gained considerable recognition. The magazine Bildende Kunst wrote: "Only the artist who can inspire the working classes to great deeds will be the true hero of his people. Did Walter Arnold's work pass this test, did it meet the people's demands? Yes, it did. [...] He understood that only with the same convinced enthusiasm as shown by our activists and heroes of labor can works be created that are firmly grounded in socialism and help that which is new and future-oriented in nature and society to break through." (Bildende Kunst, 1953, no. 1, p. 49–50)

With works such as *Youth—Master Builder of the GDR* from 1951 or *Female Tractor Operator* from 1953, Arnold contributed significantly to the desired image of the still nascent GDR. In addition to these bronzes, the artist created wooden sculptures, especially in his late works, which was unusual in the late 1960s. Among these works is *Forward and Never Forget—Solidarity*. In contrast to the bronzes, which were modelled in great detail, Arnold worked these figures out of the block as high relief only roughly and expressively, leaving the traces of processing visible. The preoccupation with the theme of 'Vietnam' was reflected repeatedly in Arnold's oeuvre. While the female figure *Vietnam Accuses*, created in the same year, could serve as a memorial, Arnold gave his group a prompting character calling directly for solidarity with Vietnam. He placed a European figure in front of a Vietnamese one as though the former were protecting the latter and had them hold each other's hands vigorously as a sign of militant support. Helmut Netzker noted: "As the title suggests, this wooden sculpture follows similar principles as the political poster. It wants to appeal, to agitate, it wants to induce the viewer to join the phalanx of solidarity." (Bildende Kunst, 1968, no. 5, p. 258).

Astrid Nielsen

Gerhard Bondzin
1930–2014

Vietnam's Trees Will Green
Again, 1965, woodcut,
61.4 × 70.7 cm

Vietnamese Mother, 1965,
woodcut, 61.3 × 70.9 cm

*Kunstfonds, Staatliche Kunstsammlungen
Dresden, inv. no. L 10406-2, L 10406-1*

The artist-functionary Gerhard Bondzin belonged to the most successful representatives of socialist realism in the GDR, who clearly declared their support for the party and the state and were given posts and privileges in return. In 1965, at the age of 35, he became a professor and at the same time rector at the Dresden Academy of Fine Arts. From 1970 to 1974, he was president of the Association of Visual Artists of the GDR. From 1971, he was active as an informant for the Ministry for State Security.

As a young lecturer, he had already traveled to Vietnam in 1962. He was interested in the landscape and people, which he captured in drawings, watercolors and paintings. "I saw the strength", he later reported, "the enthusiasm of the Vietnamese people to overcome all the sad legacies of colonialism." Since that trip, which was to be followed by a second in 1979, he took a lively interest in the fate of the country. When the Vietnam War escalated in the mid-1960s, the Afro-Asian Solidarity Committee of the GDR formed a Vietnam Committee, of which Bondzin was a member from the beginning. At the Dresden Academy, he founded a Vietnam Committee and organized many solidarity activities.

In 1964/65, he created a series of five woodcuts in which he denounced the war crimes of the USA and depicted the suffering and struggle of the Vietnamese people. In accordance with the official political reading of this war in the GDR, Bondzin shows the overpowering aggressor on one side, attacking with chemical warfare agents (Agent Orange, napalm bombs) and massive bombardments (Rolling Thunder), and the defending, 'heroically fighting people' on the other side, outgunned but carried by an 'unbroken will to win'. The enormous military aid provided by the Soviet Union and China to Vietnam's communists is of course absent from this narrative. The illustrative-decorative style of the graphics also contains clichés and stereotypes (clothing, faces). Bondzin's Vietnam cycle achieved significant popularity in the GDR and was frequently exhibited and published. It is a prime example of pictorial propaganda against Western imperialism. Two of these prints were reproduced by the Vietnam Committee in an edition of 5,000 each to be sold at solidarity auctions and distributed as thanks for donations.

Mathias Wagner

Hartwig Ebersbach b. 1940

Dedication to Chile, 1974,
oil on hardboard, 12 panels,
6 panels each 200 × 60 cm,
6 panels each 120 × 60 cm

Ludwig Forum Aachen, Ludwig Collection,
Donation Peter and Irene Ludwig

In the GDR, relations with socialist Chile under Salvador Allende, the worldwide condemnation of the military coup of September 1973, and sympathy for the fate of the Chilean people played a special role, which was repeatedly reflected in the visual arts until the 1980s. Hartwig Ebersbach's Dedication to Chile stands out from the many works created on this topic because it is a superbly painted and timeless remembrance of the victims of political conflicts.

The artist used a police photograph from the time of the Paris Commune of 1871 as a model, showing twelve executed communards displayed in lined-up coffins on the street. Ebersbach rendered this motif into a twelve-part painting by painting each of the dead on a separate panel, the narrow vertical formats resembling the coffins. He translated the unemotional documentation of the black-and-white photograph into a dynamically gestural painting of expressive color, in which the red paint coagulates like blood and recalls the drama of violent death. By juxtaposing the present (Chile coup) and the past (Paris Commune), Ebersbach shines a light on a recurring theme of history: the fate of those people who had fought for a better life and suffered persecution, torture, and death.

But *Dedication to Chile* should not be understood only as an expression of grief and empathy. For Ebersbach, this work also embodied the *Principle of Hope* formulated by Ernst Bloch (and published in the GDR in 1954), according to which, in the future, ultimately "even those who have failed [...] can be triumphant, victors of history." In the exhibition space, the picture panels are presented in two rows, one behind the other, standing on the floor and leaning against the wall so that those who were murdered face us standing upright, seemingly admonishing us. This spatial situation marks Ebersbach's first attempt to "move into space with painting," from which he developed his concept of an installative painting.

Mathias Wagner

On Guard, 1961, woodcut in
two colors, 95 × 42 cm

Cuban Mother, 1963, woodcut,
96 × 24 cm

Kupferstich-Kabinett, Staatliche
Kunstsammlungen Dresden,
inv. no. A 1965-200, A 1965-223

Copperplate engravings were already being produced in Cuba as early as the 18th century, but it was not until the 19th century that graphic art experienced a golden age in Cuban workshops. Primarily through the technique of lithography, traditional cultural practices were depicted in the sense of costumbrismo (popular painting), as well as landscapes and city views, and the burgeoning tobacco industry. In the first half of the 20th century, the focus shifted towards painting and sculpture until Cuban artists revived graphic art from the 1950s onwards.

As initiator and president of the Asociación de Grabadores de Cuba (Association of Cuban Graphic Artists, AGC for short, 1950–1968), founded in 1950, Carmelo Gónzalez was one of the practitioners who gave graphics as an art form a prominent profile in Cuba and in the international context. Inspired by the Mexican school and the Taller de Gráfica Popular, founded in Mexico City in 1937, Cuban graphic art defined itself as a political instrument that visually manifested and ideologically supported the Cuban Revolution (1953–1959).

The predominantly monochrome woodcuts by Gónzalez shown in the exhibition were created between 1961 and 1963. The slender vertical format takes its cue from the verticality of the human body, which is often used as a central pictorial motif. The visual confluence of body and urban landscape is striking, e. g. in the sheet *On Guard*, which narrates stations of Cuban history inside the silhouette of the soldier.

The imagery, charged with national and militant symbols—almost every image shows a weapon—underscores the militant intention that emanates from the artists and is meant to be transmitted to the beholder. The aesthetics of Gónzalez's woodcuts differ significantly from the graphic art of the non-governmental organization OSPAAAL, founded in 1966, which has accelerated the technical printing process through offset and silkscreen printing and is characterized by strong, bright colors (p. 100–101).

Lena Geuer

Lea Grundig 1906–1977

Shanghai (Women Reading in the Habor of Shanghai), 1960, pen and ink, watercolors, 41.6 × 59.4 cm

Kupferstich-Kabinett, Staatliche Kunstsammlungen Dresden, inv. No. C 1975-14

In 1960, a five-week study trip through the People's Republic of China took the graphic artist Lea Grundig to Beijing, Shanghai and villages in the provinces around Wuhan and Hangzhou. As a professor at the Dresden Academy of Fine Arts and later president of the Association of Visual Artists of the GDR, Grundig was able to undertake various trips abroad, including to China, Cuba, Romania and Cambodia. During her trip to China, she produced ink drawings of workers, party functionaries, and children, as well as several landscapes. After her return, the prints were exhibited in the Pavillon der Kunst (Pavilion of Art) in Berlin. As Lea Grundig wrote in the booklet accompanying the exhibition, they were intended to depict the "growth of the whole people," i.e. the development of the People's Republic under Mao Zedong, "through the eyes of a communist," without romanticizing it. For example, the drawing *Shanghai (Women Reading in the Habor of Shanghai)* shows a group of women workers reading books during their break. They symbolize emancipation and new educational opportunities for women under communism. Some drawings are accompanied by biographical details that illustrate how the revolution improved the lives of those depicted. Contemporary exhibition reviews in the GDR praised the humanity and realism of the portraits as well as Grundig's casual and vivid style.

After the two states had been founded in 1949 within a few days of each other, the People's Republic of China was initially an important political partner for the GDR. The cultural agreement signed in 1952 provided for reciprocal visits and study trips by visual artists. However, due to disagreements with the Soviet Union and the beginning of the Chinese Cultural Revolution, the exchange increasingly dried up in the 1960s. Lea Grundig's prints thus bear witness to the cultural understanding and friendship between the GDR and the People's Republic of China that was initially intended.

Nora Kaschuba

Struggle with Death, 1988,
acrylic on hardboard,
110.5 × 185 cm

Kustodie der Hochschule für Bildende
Künste Dresden, inv. no. A 0165

Born to Palestinian parents in Sabha, Libya, and raised in Syria, Mohamed Saleh Khalil was delegated by the Palestine Liberation Organization (PLO) to study art in the GDR, where he was one of about 50 students from countries of the Global South to receive training at the Dresden Academy of Fine Arts. In 1981, Khalil first attended the obligatory German course at the Herder Institute in Leipzig. Between 1982 and 1988, he studied painting and graphic arts with Professor Jutta Damme and others in Dresden, where he received his diploma in 1988. The graphic part of the final submission was the artist's book *Sabra* with 20 etchings by Khalil, which complement poems by the Palestinian poet Mahmoud Darwish. They are dedicated to the bloody three-day massacres of Sabra and Shatila, which began on September 16, 1982, when primarily Christian militias attacked the Palestinian refugee camps of Sabra and Shatila in Beirut at the height of the civil war in Lebanon. Hundreds of Palestinians and many Lebanese were killed and experienced violence and trauma. Moved by the fate of the victims, Khalil places this at the center of his final submission, which also includes three paintings. In the painting *Struggle with Death*, Khalil refers to the brutal massacre and the terrible experiences of the people. In an implied landscape, two groups of figures face each other, their fear and struggle for survival expressed through looks, gestures and emotions.

Pauline Hohn

Frieder Heinze b. 1950
Olaf Wegewitz b. 1949

ŭnāulŭtŭ—Little Stones in the Sand, 1985–86, artist's book with 68 graphics, facsimile drawings and texts, mixed media, 51 × 45 × 9 cm

Kupferstich-Kabinett, Staatliche Kunstsammlungen Dresden, inv. no. B 1986-10

The handmade artist's book *unāulŭtŭ—Little Stones in the Sand* was created in collaboration with numerous craft workshops between 1985 and 1986. It was published in a split edition of 135 copies simultaneously by the Leipzig publishing house Reclam Verlag and by the West Berlin gallery Brusberg. It combines materials from various places to create a multi-layered work: up to four pages can be unfolded next to each other, allowing for spatial expansion; the bullroarer that serves as a ribbon bookmark or grains of rice in the binding add an acoustic dimension when the book is handled.

The starting point of *unāulŭtŭ* is the artists' interest in drawings by the Karajá, which the ethnologist Fritz Krause had commissioned from members of the community during an expedition in Brazil between 1908 and 1909 and collected in a sketchbook. Krause wrote the title "unāulŭtŭ" next to one of the drawings; it was later translated as 'little stones in the sand'. Heinze and Wegewitz were able to examine the notes in Leipzig's Grassi Museum.

At the center of the artist's book is the intended dialogue between his own graphic works and the enlarged facsimiles of sketches by the Karajá. They are complemented by epic, lyrical, and essayistic texts, as well as a creation story from the Amazon region collected by the Hungarian ethnologist Lajos Boglár. In Wegewitz's words, the book's intention was "to attempt to proclaim an openness towards other cultures from within the GDR". For the artists, working with the drawings of the Karajá even offered the possibility of an imagined journey and engagement with cultural influences beyond the experiences they were able to gather in

their Leipzig homeland. The desired pictorial dialog is based on the aesthetic, comparative perception of the Karajá culture by the two artists, which they also approached through background research, as the extensive text section illustrates. In the 1980s in particular, 'the other' was an important reference point for artists in the GDR in order to distance themselves from the normative society and open up free spaces, especially by bridging geographical borders. From today's perspective, this reference becomes clear in its specific ambivalence and is also subject to criticism.

Regardless of this, *unāulŭtŭ* is an outstanding testimony to the artistic book production of the time and demonstrates in an exemplary way the search of artists in the GDR for inspiration and stimulation beyond the prevailing cultural policy and despite limited travel opportunities.

Pauline Hohn, Jule Lagoda

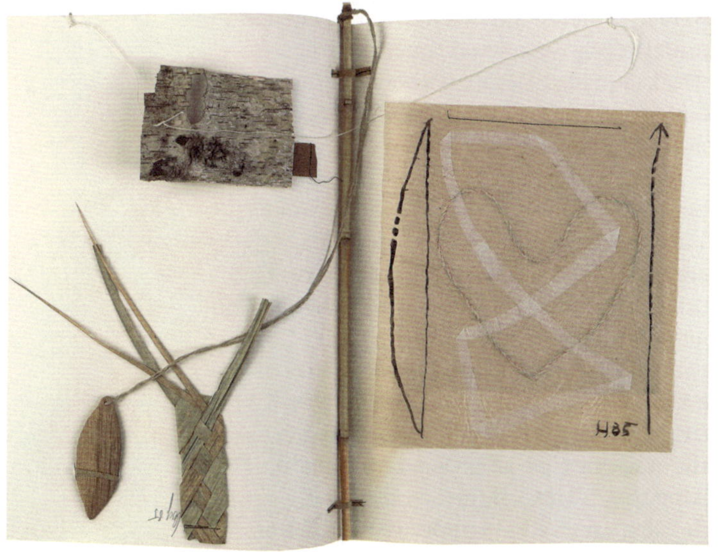

Sven Johne b. 1976

The City of Vinh, 2009,
24 pigment inkjet prints on
cotton paper, frame: each
31.6 × 41.8 cm, installation:
126.4 × 250.8 × 3 cm

Kunststiftung DZ Bank

In the work of Sven Johne, two levels are irritatingly juxtaposed: archival material and artistic photography, the past and the present. How the photographs from 2009 and the texts relate to each other is not immediately apparent. The texts are the captions on the back of the historical ADN press photos of the GDR from the 1970s of the construction of the city of Vinh, which provided the official interpretation and were used in publications. In contrast, Johne's photographs show ageing, dilapidated buildings, almost completely covered with sprawling vegetation.

After destruction during the Vietnam War, Vinh was rebuilt in the 1970s. Many East Bloc countries, including the GDR, supported the project as part of a unique large-scale reconstruction program. In addition to the 'revolutionary struggle against the destructive forces of imperialism', it was also intended as an architectural demonstration of the efficiency and innovative power of socialism.

The reconstruction of the completely destroyed city was to reorganize people's lives: a modern city for the new, socialist human being. The residential complexes, which were considered 'luxurious', were to house mainly the workers and functionaries who had made a significant contribution to nation-building. Vinh became the most modern city in the country.

The ravages of time eroded not only the buildings but also the promises and utopias. The greenery around the residential complexes—once part of the architecture's progressive planning with natural shading and ventilation—seems to devour the decaying structures. Sven Johne speaks of an "overgrown utopia." Since the 1990s, the perception of the buildings had changed: they were by then considered outdated. After the collapse of the Soviet Union, socialist architecture underwent a kind of 'pathologization': the buildings, considered unsightly or untidy, were now to make way for new high-rises. What do the images of the city of Vinh tell us today?

Martin Buhlig

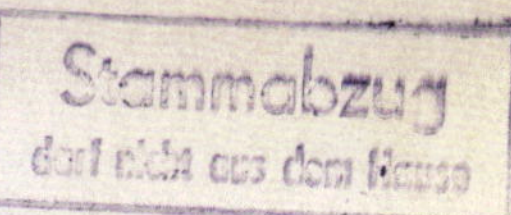

II Viet EIIIa4a

1974

ADN-ZB/HAGEN/22.10.1974/kre/DRV: Neue Wohnviertel entstehen in
VINH / Fünf Monate nach der Grundsteinlegung wächst in VINH,
der Bezirkshauptstadt der Provinz Nghe An, der erste Gebäude-
komplex mit sechs fünfgeschossigen Neubauten an der Straße
Quang Trung heran (unser Foto).
Die während der USA-Aggression gegen das vietnamesiche Volk
fast völlig zerstörte Stadt wird entsprechend einem Regierungs-
abkommen zwischen der DDR und der DRV mit Unterstützung von
Spezialisten aus der DDR, die bei der Projektierung, Planung,
Technologie und Organisation sowie bei der Qualifizierung
vietnamesischer Fachleute helfen, wiederaufgebaut.
N 1022/22 N

(Siehe dazu ADN-Meldung vom 22.10.1974)

Martha Ketsela b. 1955

The Happiness of the Earth, portfolio with aphorisms and woodcuts, 1980, 53.4 × 31 cm

Kupferstich-Kabinett, Staatliche Kunstsammlungen Dresden, inv. no.-No. B 2018-15

In the late 1970s, there was a diplomatic rapprochement between Ethiopia and the GDR, that culminated in a cultural agreement in 1977 and entailed various exchange efforts between the two countries in the field of art. In the graphic portfolio *The Happiness of the Earth* by Martha Ketsela, they materialize literally. Her work centers on people and their actions in their environment—illustrated in short aphorisms or words of wisdom. These are reproduced side by side on each sheet in Amharic (one of the most widely spoken languages in Ethiopia) and German, illustrated with abstract motifs.

Individual areas of saturated color are combined to form a pictorial theme, occasionally interrupted by delicate white lines, which, as indentations in the relief printing, refer to the use of woodcuts.

Martha Ketsela, who moved from the Ethiopian capital, Addis Ababa, to the GDR for a six-month internship as part of the cultural agreement, created a series of six graphic sheets. At the Dresden Academy of Fine Arts, she worked mainly in the printing workshops, together with the lecturer and artist Hernando León, among others. *The Hapiness of the Earth* was printed in an edition of 15 copies. Until now, it has received little attention, although the artwork is both: a historical testimony and a personal perspective on the international relations of the GDR. It raises the question of the extent to which the artist incorporated her own transcultural experiences into the work. Do the aphorisms have the same

meaning in both languages? By using the
aphorisms, their translations and illustrations,
Ketsela seems to be trying to build a bridge
of understanding between Ethiopia and the
GDR by artistic means.

Jule Lagoda

1

2

3

4

Hamlet Lavastida b. 1983

1 Memoria del Hospital Psiquiátrico de la Habana, José Lezama Lima (Memory of the psychiatric hospital of Havana)

2 Unidades Militares de Ayuda a la Producción (UMAP) (Military units to support production)

3 Brigada Especial, Villa Marista, Cien y Aldabo, El Vivac (State security service)

4 Congreso Nacional de Educación y Cultura 1971, Heberto Padilla (National congress of education and culture)

From the series *Cultura Profiláctica* (Culture of Prevention), 2020–2021, paper cuts, each 100 × 70 cm

Courtesy of the artist

"[There are] basically two options—jail or exile—for Cuban artists in cultural artivism." These were the words Hamlet Lavastida used last year to describe the grim reality for artists and intellectuals in Cuba. He himself was expatriated in early 2022 after three months in prison and deported to Europe. Due to numerous human rights violations, the economy of scarcity, and strict censorship, the Cuban diaspora has grown significantly in recent years.

In his work cycle *Cultura Profiláctica* (Culture of Prevention), the artist points to the continuity of a policy of surveillance and repression in totalitarian-ruled Cuba that began with the Cuban Revolution and continues to this day. His white paper cuts presented on a colored background are mainly based on symbols, emblems, and abbreviations of political and social organizations, some of which he combines with figures of well-known personalities. At first,

these pictorial elements create the impression of a decorative and harmless surface, but underneath, Lavastida exposes Cuba's repressive system. In addition to open violence, the Cuban government's most important political instrument for combating the opposition is the exercise of power through institutions. UMAP, for example, stands for Unidades Militares de Ayuda a la Producción (Military Units to Support Production). This term refers specifically to a labor and concentration camp that existed from 1965 to 1968 in the province of Camagüey, where gay men, opposition members, and others were tortured and forced to work. The Brigada Especial resembles the Ministry of State Security (known as Stasi) in the GDR and serves to monitor people critical of the government. By transferring the original images into monochrome paper cuts composed of photographs and the design of various logos, the artist creates a unified aesthetic. This exemplifies how dictatorial regimes require all individuals to submit to the ideology of the revolution—including the intellectuals José Lezama Lima and Heberto Padilla, whose work has been censored by the state. The case of the writer Padilla, who in 1971 submitted his self-accusation in a public letter after weeks of psychological torture, caused a rethink among intellectuals outside Cuba who had previously supported the Cuban Revolution.

Lena Geuer

Heinz Lohmar 1900–1976

Congo Triptych, 1965,
oil on hardboard,
left panel 123 × 100 cm,
centre panel 170 × 125 cm,
right panel 125 × 101 cm

Albertinum, Staatliche Kunstsammlungen
Dresden, Gal. no. 68/16

The *Congo Triptych* painted by Heinz Lohmar in 1965 is set in the context of the documentaries *Kommando 52, Der lachende Mann*, and *PS zum lachenden Mann*, which Walter Heynowski and Peter Hellmich or Studio H&S made between 1965 and 1966 using West German media footage (p. 63–70). The films triggered an extensive press campaign; like Lohmar's work, they denounced the bloody conflict of the so-called Congo Crisis and West German neocolonialism.

In the center panel *That Was a Man*, a position in which Christian tradition would have a figure on the cross, a decapitated and tortured Black corpse is shown. A second corpse, its bulging red lips invoking racist stereotypes, stares dead-eyed at the audience.

On the left panel—*The Hero of the Western World*—the perpetrators of these inhuman crimes can be seen. The then prime minister of the post-colonial Democratic Republic of Congo, Moïse Tshombé, was supported by the West by way of white mercenaries, with the approval of the United States and Belgium. In the latter figure, surrounded by representatives from politics, the military and business, as well as prostitutes, two persons merge into one: the West German Major Siegfried Müller, head of the mercenary command 52, and the Belgian Lieutenant Mazy.

This image is mirrored by the right panel *They Reaped Storm*. Black people raise clenched fists in the air. The only female

person, Pauline Opango Lumumba, wife of the assassinated first prime minister Patrice Lumumba, is presented with her upper body exposed. She had led a protest march to United Nations headquarters bare-chested; Lohmar, however, shows the activist in a pin-up pose. Two men lead the group. A *white* and a Black figure arranged as a pair of brothers in solidarity join forces in the liberation struggles of the Global South. True to this spirit, Lohmar donated his fee to the Vietnam Solidarity Fund.[1] On the one hand, the *Congo Triptych* opens up its visual space to the concerns of Congolese people. On the other hand, however, the protagonists are staged as if only capable of acting in the context of the Soviet empire.

Petra Lange-Berndt

1   Willi Zahlbaum, secretary of the Afro-Asian Solidarity Committee in the German Democratic Republic, Berlin, to Gerhard Bondzin, rector of the Dresden Academy of Fine Arts, dated 17.9.1965, Archiv der Hochschule für Bildende Künste Dresden, Bestand 03, Sign. 03/437.

Dana Lorenz b. 1984

Re-Writing Gaze, 2018,
2-channel video installation
of five HD videos in super
slow motion, with sound
collages, Lisa - 5:57 min,
Muna - 22:28 min, Henni
13:23 min, Woudy - 6:15 min,
Lai - 13:41 min

Courtesy of the artist

The video piece *Re-Writing Gaze* shows five portrait situations of people who open up a sensual-physical space in an intimate gaze relationship with the artist Dana Lorenz.

The smoldering sound collage creates its own associative space beyond image and language—through sustained overlays, warm sounds morph into dull rumblings or tremors, heavy wing beats or tinnitus-like signals. The larger-than-life projections, their apparent inertia, and the sound, which constantly remixes and overlaps, create a direct and intense encounter. Unlike in painting or photography, the portraits are not stilled; the protagonists look back at the viewers with self-confidence in a re-appropriation of the gaze—who is looking at whom here?

Dana Lorenz's film portraits engage in a silent dialogue with the viewers. This interaction takes place in the exchange of glances. The subjects look resigned, optimistic, or frightened. Sometimes, the focused gaze sparkles critically and makes us aware of the superficial, canonized readings and attributions of our collective pictorial memory. We encounter protagonists who, each in their own diversity, embody a complex, transcultural self-understanding and a unique gender that is fluid and individual.

Based on the theory of the female gaze and the symbolic dimension of the 'gaze regime' (according to the art historian and director Kaja Silverman), the artist subtly questions the power dynamics of looking and being looked at. In their mimetic and inverse ways, the charged, staged changes of gaze also serve to motivate questions about the looking subject: from which position do we look? Which standardized or instinctive habits of seeing and reading, attributions, or classifications shape our encounters with other people?

In the title of the piece, the artist poses the question of the extent to which these rehearsed attitudes can be reconfigured, revised, or rewritten.

Dana Lorenz, Martin Buhlig

Mankew Valente Mahumana
1934–2021

The People in 1974, 1974,
oil on hardboard,
96.2 × 95.7 cm

GRASSI Museum für Völkerkunde zu Leipzig, inv. no. MAf 35331

"I am a realistic creative painter; that is to say, I am very close to the surrealist universe." (Mankew V. Mahumana)

The eyes fixed on two colonial soldiers are pleading, accusing, waiting. So tightly do the figures surround the soldiers, crowded into a square, that no movement and no consolation seem possible without liberation from colonial rule.

When Mankew V. Mahumana painted the image in 1974, Mozambique was worn out by ten years of war between the FRELIMO liberation front and the Portuguese colonial power. The artist saw his purpose in using his paintings to fight for the emancipation of his people. On June 25, 1975, Mozambique gained independence. Together with other Mozambican artists such as Malangatana Valente Ngwenya and João Craveirinha, Mankew created a new visual language to confidently depict the future of a socialist Mozambique.

In the course of the 1980s, the GDR became one of Mozambique's most important international partners, a fact that was reflected in the cultural and visual cosmos of both countries. Works of art from Mozambique were presented in the Ausstellungszentrum am Fernsehturm Berlin (Exhibition Center at the Berlin Television Tower), DEFA films were shown even in remote provinces of Mozambique, and educational exchanges were made possible. In 1983, Mankew was appointed a corresponding member of the Academy of Arts of the German Democratic Republic. That same year, he created a mural in Mozambique honoring the support of East German workers in constructing the Moatize mining center. Mankew used such propagandistic works to promote economic cooperation between the GDR and Mozambique.

"Only a relationship of equality and cooperation can make freedom possible," Mankew wrote in a letter to the Academy of Arts of the German Democratic Republic. As a corresponding member, he used his voice to call for equal recognition of Mozambican artists whose style was fundamentally different from the socialist realism in the art of the GDR.

Lea Marie Nienhoff

César Olhagaray
b. 1951

Black and White, 1979,
oil on canvas, 105 × 140 cm

Kustodie der Hochschule für Bildende
Künste Dresden, inv. no. A 0520

The painting *Black and White* by the artist César Olhagaray, who now lives in Dresden and Santiago de Chile, was created in 1979, one year before he received his diploma. He had already been in the GDR since 1974, when he had to leave his native Chile due to the military coup on September 11, 1973 and his subsequent imprisonment. The GDR, where he emigrated after a brief stay in France, offered Olhagaray political asylum. Between 1974 and 1980, he studied painting and graphic arts at the Dresden Academy of Fine Arts, where he was one of only six Chilean students until 1990. His teachers included Hernando León, himself trained at the Dresden Academy in the 1960s, who taught many students from countries of the Global South.

In Chile, Olhagaray had already been a member of mural brigades that produced paintings with revolutionary content throughout the country. He continued this work in the GDR and contributed to murals in Dresden, Rostock, Erfurt and Berlin, among other cities. Again and again, solidarity, as well as the stand against the Pinochet dictatorship, were at the center of his work. But his artistic work was also influenced by dance, performance, theater and architecture, as well as the exchange with the public, and to this day, it is influenced by a collective approach.

With *Black and White*, which was created when he was still at art academy, Olhagaray created a work full of antagonisms, and not just because of the black and white contrast: the abstract-cubist forms are juxtaposed with random spray techniques, both of which contradict the state-propagated representationalism in art, which was also the standard at the art academy at the time.

Pauline Hohn

1 **Daysi Garciá López**
Day of Solidarity with
African-American People/
August 18, 1969, offset print,
55 × 43.5 cm

2 **Olivio Martínez Viera**
Guatemala—Day of Solidarity
with Guatemala, february 6,
1968, offset print, 55 × 34.5 cm

3 **Daysi Garciá López**
Angola—Solidarity Day,
4 February, 1969, offset print,
54 × 33 cm

4 **Jesús Forjans Boade**
Day of Solidarity with Laos
October 12, 1968,
offset print, 55 × 33 cm

Kupferstich-Kabinett, Staatliche
Kunstsammlungen Dresden,
inv. no. A 2021-41, A 2021-42,
A 2021-38, A 2021-40

García López, Alfredo G. Rostgaard
and Elena Serrano designed more than 400
posters for the magazine until its discon-
tinuation in 2019 (total circulation: more than
nine million). Stylistically, they drew on
American Pop Art, Afro-Cuban symbolism,
psychedelic art, and commercial advertising.
Using bright colors and strong contrasts,
they translated the solidarity messages and
calls to arms into universally understandable
images. They designed memorable figures,
used patriotic symbols, typical folkloric
pictorial elements and national colors, and
employed photography and constructivist
montage. The result was an immediate
imagery that reached people who could not
read or write. The frequently used symbolism
of weapons corresponded to the awareness
of living in a time of permanent resistance
and struggle of the oppressed peoples, with
OSPAAAL seeing itself as their pacemaker.

Mathias Wagner

In January 1966, the Solidarity Organization
with the Peoples of Asia, Africa and Latin
America (Organización de Solidaridad de los
Pueblos de Asia, África y América Latina,
OSPAAAL) was founded in Havana. Its goal
was to coordinate solidarity among the
young nation-states and freedom movements
that had become independent on all three
continents and to strengthen socialist
internationalism. OSPAAAL propagated the
worldwide struggle against imperialism,
colonialism and racism, was committed to
the anti-apartheid movement in South
Africa and opposed the U.S. war in Vietnam.
From 1967 on, the organization published
the magazine TRIcontinental with articles
on political, economic and cultural perspectives of the Global South. It had Spanish,
English, French and Arabic editions and was
distributed worldwide (though not in the
GDR). The initial print run was 50,000 copies.
Each issue was accompanied by a folded
poster calling for solidarity with individual
countries, movements or personalities.
Cuban artists such as Gladys Acosta Ávila,
Félix Beltrán, Jesús Forjans Boade, Daysi

Jornada de Solidaridad con el pueblo Afroamericano/18 de agosto
Day of Solidarity with the Afro-American People/August 18
Journée de Solidarité avec le peuple Afro-américain/le 18 août
OSPAAAL

1

Guatemala
Jornada de Solidaridad con Guatemala   6 de febrero
Day of Solidarity with Guatemala   february 6
Journée de Solidarité avec le Guatemala   6 février
OSPAAAL

2

angola
Jornada de Solidaridad
Day of Solidarity
Journée de Solidarité
4 Febrero/February/Février
OSPAAAL

3

OSPAAAL
JORNADA DE SOLIDARIDAD CON LAOS OCTUBRE 12 - DAY OF
SOLIDARITY WITH LAOS OCTOBER 12 - JOURNEE DE SOLIDARITE
AVEC LAOS 12 OCTOBRE -

4

Margarita Pellegrin
1940–2016

Demonstration, 1977,
wool, cotton, knotted,
128 × 145 cm

Kunstgewerbemuseum, Staatliche
Kunstsammlungen Dresden,
inv. no. 50383

As her tapestry *Demonstration* illustrates, Margarita Pellegrin's work is dominated by a vivid use of color and an ornamental visual vocabulary that was profoundly influenced by her encounter with the carpet weaving of Chile's indigenous peoples. Besides painting and graphic art, Pellegrin's artistic practice included textile art and exemplifies the transcultural interconnection between the GDR and Chile.

Born in Aue, Margarita Pellegrin studied at the Arbeiter- und Bauernfakultät (Workers' and Farmers' Faculty) of the Dresden Academy of Fine Arts from 1958 to 1961. There she met the artist Hernando León, her future husband, whom she would follow to his native Chile in 1963. From 1964 to 1974, Pellegrin worked as an assistant in the Graphics Department and a lecturer in Design at the Universidad de Chile in the northern town of Antofagasta. There, she was part of a circle of artists whose friendship and collaboration continued after 1973 in Dresden. The military coup in Chile on September 11, 1973, caused thousands to flee and also caused the artist and her husband to return to the GDR, where they both worked as freelance artists in Dresden.

In her art, Pellegrin often explored what it means to be human in the world. After 1973, her art often references the military coup d'état in Chile. Thus, the protest of the group of figures in the tapestry is most certainly directed against the dictatorial regime under Augusto Pinochet and the brutal persecution of the dissident Chileans. In its powerful color tone, it is at the same time an expression of the people's unbroken will to live.

Pauline Hohn

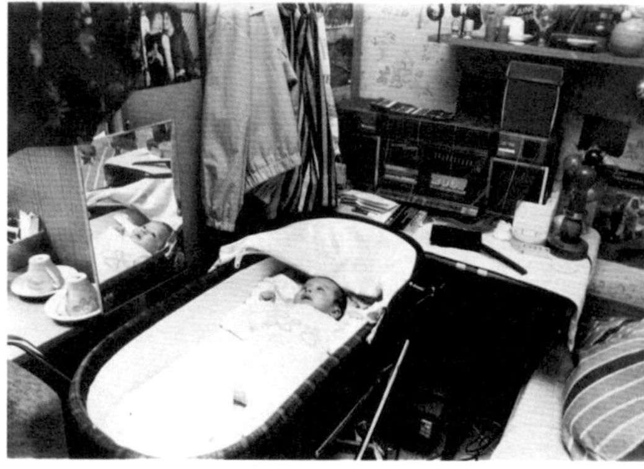

Matthias Rietschel
b. 1958

From the series *Vietnamese in Dresden,* 1987–1990, b/w photographs, each 32.8 × 47.8 cm

Kunstfonds, Staatliche Kunstsammlungen Dresden, inv. no. 96/5/91, 96/7/91, 96/9/91, 96/11/91, 96/16/91, 96/17/91, 96/22/91, 96/23/91

The photographer Matthias Rietschel, a graduate of the Academy of Fine Arts Leipzig, belongs to the generation that used its artistic means to take a close look at the social conditions of the GDR and their distortions.

In 1989, he received a commission in Dresden on the subject of *Foreign Workers in the GDR—a Photo Documentary on Work, Leisure and Friendship.* Rietschel had become interested in the subject after meeting Vietnamese people living in a dormitory in Dresden, and had already taken first photographs before the commission was awarded. In 1991, the photographer compiled a selection of 32 prints for the Kunstfonds, showing scenes from life in the dormitory as well as everyday work life at VEB Herren-mode Dresden (men's fashion state-owned company), which acted as the photogra-pher's 'social partner' in this commissioned work. The factory had been employing Vietnamese, who had come to the GDR for a limited period of time as 'contract workers' under a bilateral government agreement, since 1987. As with other foreign workers in the GDR, their stay was strictly regulated, even in the private sphere. Wherever possible, contact with locals was prevented (even by the authorities), but in everyday life they often managed to live together as colleagues and friends. If he had stuck to the official rules, Rietschel's photo series could not have existed in this form. On the one hand, he needed special permission to move around freely with his camera in the company and in the dormitory. On the other hand, many of the motifs, which testify to great closeness and trust as well as individual observation and sympathy, would not have been con-ceivable without close personal contact.

With this look behind the scenes of the official narrative, characterized by subjective authenticity, Matthias Rietschel makes an important contribution to the social panorama of the late GDR. At the same time, the photo essay became an unplanned documentation of the fate of the Vietnamese 'contract workers' immediately after the fall of the Berlin Wall.

Silke Wagler

Sonya Schönberger b. 1975

Braised Heart, 2022, video,
sound, 29 min

Courtesy of the artist

As a Fellow of the research project *Art in Networks— The GDR and its Global Relations* at the TUD Dresden University of Technology and a Fellow of the artist residency Villa Aurora in Los Angeles in 2022, Sonya Schönberger explored the Wende Museum in Culver City, which houses an extensive collection of artifacts from the former GDR. For the resulting video work *Braised Heart*, Schönberger collaborated with playwright Enis Maci, who stayed at Villa Aurora at the same time as her.

The camera looks over Maci's shoulder as she observes and associatively comments on a series of objects in the collection. These are private as well as official relics from the 'socialist dream liner' MS Völkerfreundschaft, which mainly sailed to socialist brother countries on Mediterranean and Black Sea voyages. Daily programs, menus, postcards, commemorative plates and a travel diary bear witness to luxurious cruises that were only possible for selected, privileged citizens of the GDR. "You can borrow binoculars, send letters, you can be entertained by the on-board band, watch a movie or buy souvenirs," Maci quotes from a 1969 brochure, then moves on to the food offered on board—including braised heart. For a moment, the 'GDR system' comes to life in these exhibits.

While Maci searches for information on the Internet and reads the history of the ship from her cell phone, we can see various texts corresponding to her improvised exploration of the materials: short definitions, a cooking recipe, advertising texts or explanations of terms (light diet, Bosporus, Cuban Crisis, the Steckenpferd movement, foreign currency, slide show, etc.), which have also obviously been 'googled'. Even the beginning of the video, in which Schönberger gives Maci the indication "It runs!" reveals both the working process and its provisionality. Not only is 'artistic research' deconstructed here, there are also references to all kinds of pseudo-expert knowledge. How can one approach history? What can artifacts convey at all? Can one go in search of truth in a museum?

Kerstin Schankweiler

Chukwuemeka Ogbue
(Student from Nigeria), 1960,
mixed media on canvas,
95.5 × 75.5 cm

Albertinum, Staatliche Kunstsammlungen
Dresden, Gal. no. 3384

From the late 1950s to the mid-1960s, Eva Schulze-Knabe from Dresden painted portraits of numerous international students, most of whom were enrolled at what was then the Technische Hochschule (now TU Dresden; University of Technology). The portraits are all executed in medium-size format, and the sitters are often shown with an open book as an attribute of learning and intellectual study. Exchange students from allied socialist countries played an important role in the foreign policy of the GDR in terms of export and international recognition.

Chukwuemeka Ogbue (born March 3, 1934 in Onicha Olona, Nigeria—died December 10, 1969 in Dresden) came to Dresden in 1957 as a student of Electrical Engineering to focus on acoustics and speech technology. He moved to East Berlin in 1962, from where he left for West Berlin due to political upheavals, returning to Dresden again in 1967 to marry his long-time partner Helga Deumert, with whom he had a son in 1961, Udoka Ogbue. In Dresden, Chukwuemeka Ogbue worked as an electrical engineer in a semi-state-owned company. In 1969, he died of a gastric rupture, which was probably diagnosed too late.

Eva Schulze-Knabe had approached Chukwuemeka Ogbue during a visit to the *Vierte Deutsche Kunstausstellung* (Fourth German Art Exhibition) at the Albertinum and invited him to sit for her portrait. The painting was acquired in 1961 from the exhibition *Neues Leben – Neue Kunst* (New Life—New Art) in the Pavillon der Kunst (Pavilion of Art) in East Berlin with funds from the GDR Kulturfonds (Cultural Fund) and has been part of the Albertinum holdings ever since.

Until 2021, the sitter's name was unknown, and the painting was known under the title *African Student*. During an exhibition on the art holdings of the TU Dresden, it was presented as a loan from the Albertinum, alongside other portraits of international students by Eva Schulze-Knabe. The son of Chukwuemeka Ogbue, who now lives in Cambridge, was made aware of his father's portrait by a friend via a film about the exhibition. Udoka Ogbue and his mother visited Dresden, where they saw the portrait again after many years and were able to provide information on the work's genesis and biography of the sitter.

Gwendolin Kremer

Wenke Seemann b. 1978

Proletarians of the GDR, Stick Stamps / We Have Fulfilled all Obligations, from the series *Solidarity, Archive Dialogues #2—Citizens*, 2022, room installation, photographs, digital print, music box, plot font, dimensions variable

Courtesy of the artist

The spatial installation gathers parts of the series *Solidarity, Archive Dialogues #2—Citizens* and presents them in a new work constellation in the context of the exhibition *Revolutionary Romances?*. A printed wallpaper shows montages of pages from East German trade union (FDGB) membership cards with collected solidarity stamps, and a statistical diagram sorts the stamps into sober numbers. How often did the support go to Chile? How often did it go to Vietnam? Next to it, a QR code directs viewers to a website with a video of a speech by playwright Heiner Müller from November 4, 1989, just a few days before the fall of the Berlin Wall, in which he accuses the FDGB of having done nothing for workers' rights in the GDR during the 40 years of its existence.

Another wall features photographs from the series *Flag Ceremony*. They document gestures of collective recognition—hands are shaken, certificates awarded. If you turn the crank of a small music box, the song *Children of the World* can be heard, which— in keeping with the state ideology—conveys ideals such as international friendship, peace and solidarity to even the youngest children.

Seemann's artistic work can be characterized as an investigative exploration of historical pictorial documents and objects. In her series *Archive Dialogues*, she deals with historical material such as photographs from her father's archive, generating constellations to explore questions of collective and individual action, social rituals and gestures from a present perspective. The artistic gaze at the intersection of historical distance and biographical reference is transferred to the ambivalence of interpretations: how significant is our social conditioning, and how does it affect our present? Are the collectively prescribed actions, such as the purchase and collecting of solidarity stamps empty propaganda rituals, is standing in formation for the flag ceremony merely indoctrination, or do they establish an understanding of the world that goes beyond the first-person perspective? And through which messages and rituals is society conveyed today?

Martin Buhlig

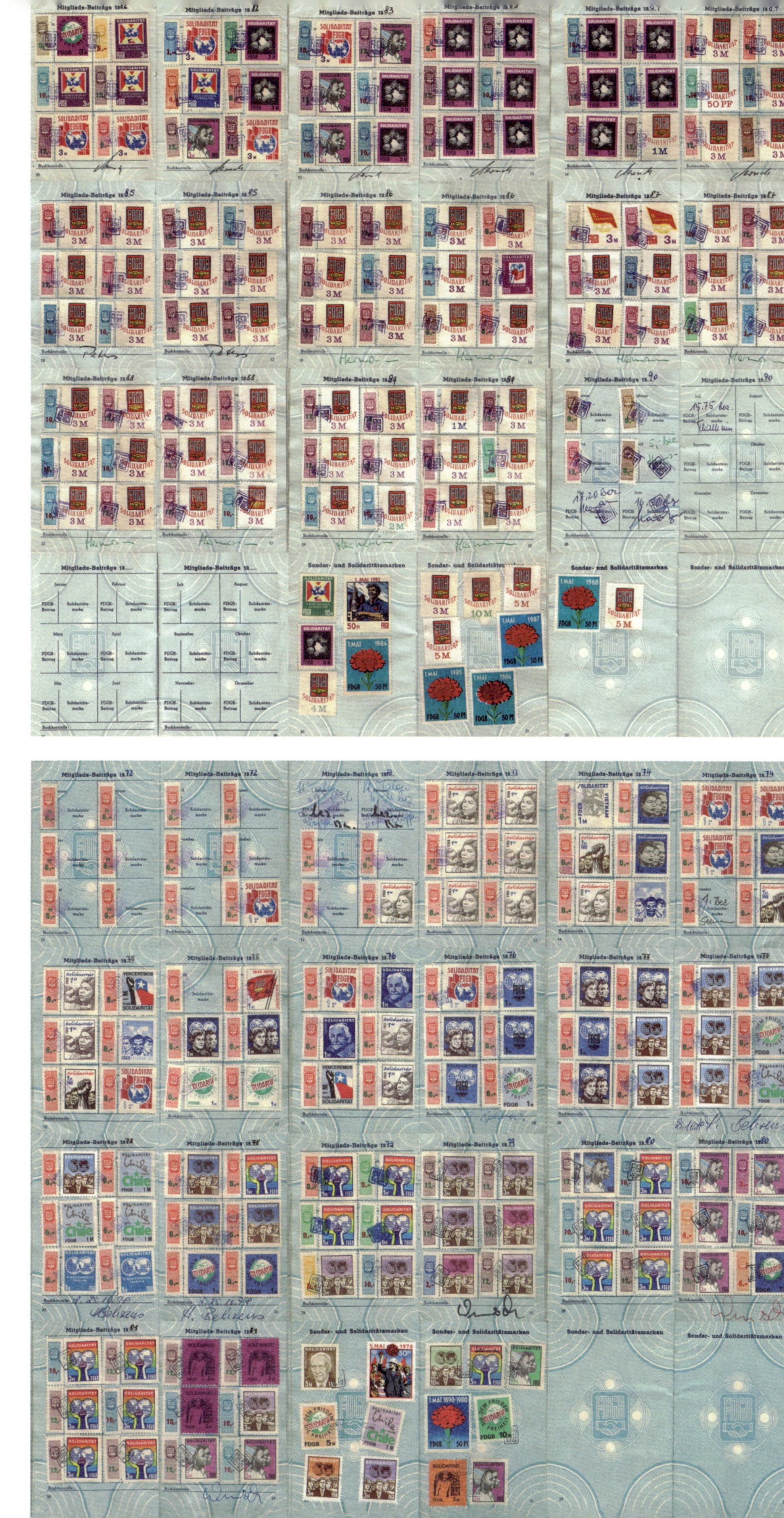

First Home, 2023, Super-8-film, digitized, 3:50 min (loop), wood-chip wallpaper

Marriage, 2023,
11 digital prints, framed,
each 32.1 × 23.4 cm

Courtesy of the artist

A projector throws Super 8 recordings onto a wall covered with woodchip wallpaper, 11 metal frames show text documents with blackened areas. As prosaic as Sung Tieu's installation initially appears, its many layers of meaning unfold when read and viewed.

While the film footage from the small town of Freital near Dresden, where Tieu spent her early childhood, seems almost nostalgic, the reproduced state security documents adopt a cool rhetoric of power revealing the extend of the strict surveillance and control exercised over the contract workers, even intruding into their private lives. Due to the 1980 recruitment agreement between the German Democratic Republic and the Socialist Republic of Vietnam, Vietnamese workers became the largest group of contract laborers in the GDR. Despite their communal living arrangements in dormitories, they often found themselves socially isolated from the broader GDR society, viewed more as a collective entity rather than as individuals.

The promised improvement in their quality of life, which contract work seemed to offer, clashed with the harsh realities of East Germany, characterized by strict sanctions, extensive control, and racial discrimination. Tieu explores the complex socio-political implications of this agreement—even beyond the fall of communism—and the psychological layering of history(s) in her work. How do living space and surroundings inscribe themselves into one's own biography? What is the relationship between subjective and collective experience? What moral parameters determine the state's external and internal actions? These questions have not lost their urgency, even when viewed from the present day.

Sung Tieu was born in Hai Duong and grew up in Freital and Berlin. In her installations, videos, sculptures with sound and text as well as in public interventions, she cites a minimalist vocabulary of forms. Research as a political practice plays a central role in her work—working with archive material, architectural stagings and found objects as an interrogation of things for their stories.

Martin Buhlig

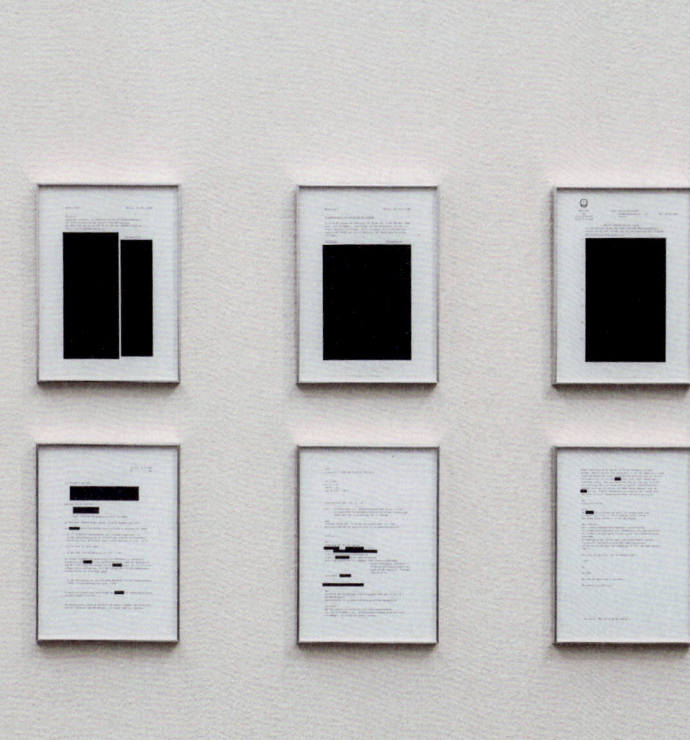

Tonel (Antonio Eligio Fernández) b. 1958

Lenin, What Is to Be Done?
1991, oil on nettle, plaka on plaster and wood, 3 parts, 200 × 200 × 25 cm

Ludwig Forum Aachen, Ludwig Collection, Loan Peter and Irene Ludwig Foundation

Two young women in bikinis are sunbathing on the beach. A man returns to the idyllic seaside resort with three fresh coconut drinks. In the background, the three of them are being watched by a statue of Lenin, which is inserted as a sculpture into the painted beach scene. Like the bust of Ernst Thälmann, which was erected in 1972 at 'Playa RDA' (Beach of the GDR) on a small Cuban island and symbolically presented to Erich Honecker by Fidel Castro in the form of a map, Cuba's ideological foster father Lenin has now also found his place in the socialist tourist paradise.

In *Lenin, What Is to Be Done?* Tonel ironically illustrates a tricky situation resulting from the special year in which the work was made, 1991. On the one hand, the Cuban art scene prospered in the 1980s, and Havana became an international art city. The *Bienal de La Habana* was founded in 1984, numerous festivals took place in the Cuban capital, and critics were full of praise for the 'New Cuban Art'. On the other hand, with the fall of the Berlin Wall and the end of the Cold War in the 1990s, the Caribbean island state was plunged into an economic and social crisis. When the Soviet Union collapsed, Cuba lost its main oil supplier. Without oil, industry could not be kept running. Castro responded with relaxations and opened Cuba to tourism. Tonel mockingly comments on this period of upheaval ('Periodo especial') in his painting by making Lenin a lifeguard and linking him visually to the new capitalist structures of the tourism industry.

The title 'Lenin, qué hacer?' refers to the 1902 pamphlet *What Is To Be Done*, by which Lenin laid the groundwork for revolutionary socialism. 'What is to be done?'—this question is thus related not only to the economic crisis but also to cultural and artistic activity in Cuba. The sandy Cuban beach, now frequented by white tourists, was repeatedly denied to Cubans themselves. As tourism grew, so did competition and racism. While Afro-Cuban culture in the 1980s was still predominantly mediated by white Cuban artists, the presence of Afro-Cuban artists increased in the 1990s—and with it the critique of racist structures in social systems.

Lena Geuer

José Toirac
b. 1966

Ever Onward to Victory, 1995,
oil on canvas, 91 × 60.5 cm

Ludwig Forum Aachen, Ludwig Collection,
Loan Peter and Irene Ludwig Foundation

The famous quote "Hasta la victoria siempre" (Ever onward to victory) was taken from the farewell letter Che Guevara is said to have addressed to Fidel Castro in 1965 before leaving Cuba for the Congo. Cuban artist José Toirac chose the quote, which has been elevated to the rallying cry of the socialist revolution, as the title of his 1995 painting. At first, it creates the impression of a photograph. Only on closer inspection do we realize that it is a painting based on a black-and-white photograph. Toirac frequently makes use of documents from Cuban state archives or illustrations from magazines and government newspapers as the basis for his works to circumvent possible censorship. We see a woman, slightly blurred, amid a crowd of people and yet elevated. The scene is reminiscent of a demonstration; the large waving flag in her hands gives the motif a revolutionary character.

Toirac lives in Cuba, and in his works, he deals with historical as well as political moments and characters in his home country, often regarding the Cuban Revolution. To expose manipulation mechanisms and power strategies, he focuses on the mostly hidden, often also concealed aspects and constructed readings. He investigates the shaping and influencing of a collective memory, which is why his work elicits harsh criticism from the state.

Pauline Hohn

Arlette Quỳnh-Anh Trần b. 1987

PLATTENLOTUS, 2022,
video, sound, 6:45 min

Courtesy of the artist

With her futuristic artistic perspective on the North Vietnamese city of Vinh, artist Arlette Quỳnh-Anh Trần's video work *PLATTEN-LOTUS* draws parallels between the years 1974 and 2074, between past, present and future, life and death, and between the Democratic Republic of Vietnam and the GDR. During the Vietnam War, Vinh was heavily destroyed by American air raids. After the war, the GDR's anti-imperialist solidarity with North Vietnam took various forms, including reconstruction aid. In Vinh, the idea of a socialist model city began to take material shape in 1974. The newly created Quang Trung housing complex with its 36 apartment blocks was designed to organize the lives of the 15,000 inhabitants as modern socialist people. The plans were drawn up by East German and Vietnamese specialists, most of whom had been trained in the GDR, but the processes of preparation and implementation did not take place on an equal footing. In addition, solutions had to be found in Vinh for the living conditions of the Vietnamese, which did not correspond to the living conditions of the East Germans.

Conceived as part of the project *Eugenics of The Cold Flowers* and developed within the framework of a fellowship of the research project *Art in Networks—The GDR and its Global Relations* at the TU Dresden (University of Technology), *PLATTENLOTUS* speculates about the future of the ideal socialist city in the year 2074 during the Qingming Festival and shows a utopian version of the interplay between architecture, collective and environment. The 1974 plan is digitally expanded in the present and used to create the hypothetical Vinh of the future. Arlette Quỳnh-Anh Trần combines experimental sound and historical sources with covert references to the destructive-spiritual by drawing a temporal link between the video and the commemoration of the dead.

Pauline Hohn

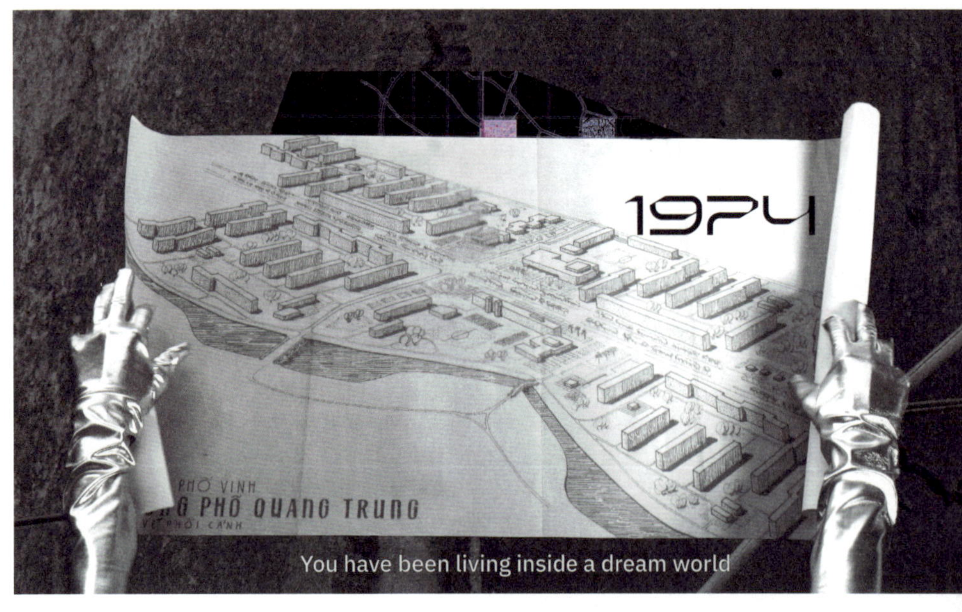

sitting on the throne

Trịnh Kim Vinh
1932–2018

Civil Defense, 1973,
color lithography,
49.9 × 59.7 cm

Kunstfonds, Staatliche Kunstsammlungen
Dresden, inv. no. 13a/1/73

Untitled (At the Steelworks),
1972, lithography,
40.5 × 55 cm

Kustodie der Hochschule für Bildende
Künste Dresden, inv. no. B 2324

Trịnh Kim Vinh joined the communist resistance movement against the French colonial power in Vietnam as a teenager. After liberation, she studied pedagogy in China and then returned to Vietnam to work as a teacher for several years. From 1964 to 1969, she studied art at Hanoi College of Fine Arts, where she learned the techniques of silk painting and woodblock printing. In 1969, two of her woodblock prints were shown at *INTERGRAFIK* in East Berlin. A year later, after taking a German course at the Herder Institute in Leipzig, she entered the Dresden Academy of Fine Arts, where she continued her studies with Gerhard Kettner (graphics) and Friderun Bondzin (painting), graduating in December 1973. In addition to learning the artistic fundamentals, her 'education plan' focused on the theory and practice of lithography. As part of the 'practice-oriented teaching' at the Dresden Academy, she interned at the VEB Rohrkombinat Stahl- und Walzwerk Riesa (sate-owned steel and rolling mill). In GDR's largest steelworks, she made sketches with motifs from everyday production and work processes, some of which she used to print lithographs. For 1973, her assignment was: "Designs and compositions on the theme of the Vietnamese liberation struggle." This resulted in a series of prints in which the artist depicts everyday life in the anti-colonial liberation war and during the Vietnam War. She was particularly interested in Vietnamese women who not only worked in industry and agriculture but also fought at the front. Five of these lithographs were exhibited in 1973 at *INTERGRAFIK* in East Berlin.

After returning to Vietnam, Trịnh Kim Vinh initially became head of the Drawing Department at the College of Fine Arts in Hanoi. In 1975, after the end of the war, she moved to the Academy of Art in Ho Chi Minh City (formerly Saigon) in South Vietnam, where she headed the Department of Sculpture and Graphic Arts and taught until her retirement in 2009.

Mathias Wagner

Christoph Wetzel
b. 1947

The Dead President, 1974,
mixed media on hardboard,
200 × 150 cm

Albertinum, Staatliche Kunstsammlungen
Dresden, inv. no. 80/13

In response to the military
coup led by General Pinochet
in Chile on September 11,
1973, Christoph Wetzel produced the painting *The Dead President*. It shows Salvador
Allende, the socialist politician and, until
the military junta, president of Chile.
The event led to a rupture in Chile's history
and the country's relations with the GDR:
the military's takeover was accompanied by
terrible violence against the opposition
movement. Despite the continuation of trade,
the GDR ended official ties and offered
asylum to some 2,000 persecuted Chileans.

With a dynamic style and deliberate
documentary authenticity, the young artist
Wetzel shows Allende slumped in an
armchair, his body draped in the Chilean
flag. No blood, no injury, not even the calm
expression on his face indicates that he
is no longer alive. Only the armchair is visibly
riddled with bullets and points to a crime,
in addition to the title. Wetzel hints at the
brutal assassination of the president by the
military and symbolizes a twofold downfall:
that of the socialist era and that of Chile's
socialist president. This follows a historiography of Allende's tragic, heroic death
that was sometimes found in the GDR press.
In fact, Allende took his own life in the face
of imminent arrest only a few hours after his
final radio address to the Chilean people on
September 11, 1973, in which he announced:
"I will leave the Moneda only as the legiti-
mate president of Chile or dead."

Pauline Hohn

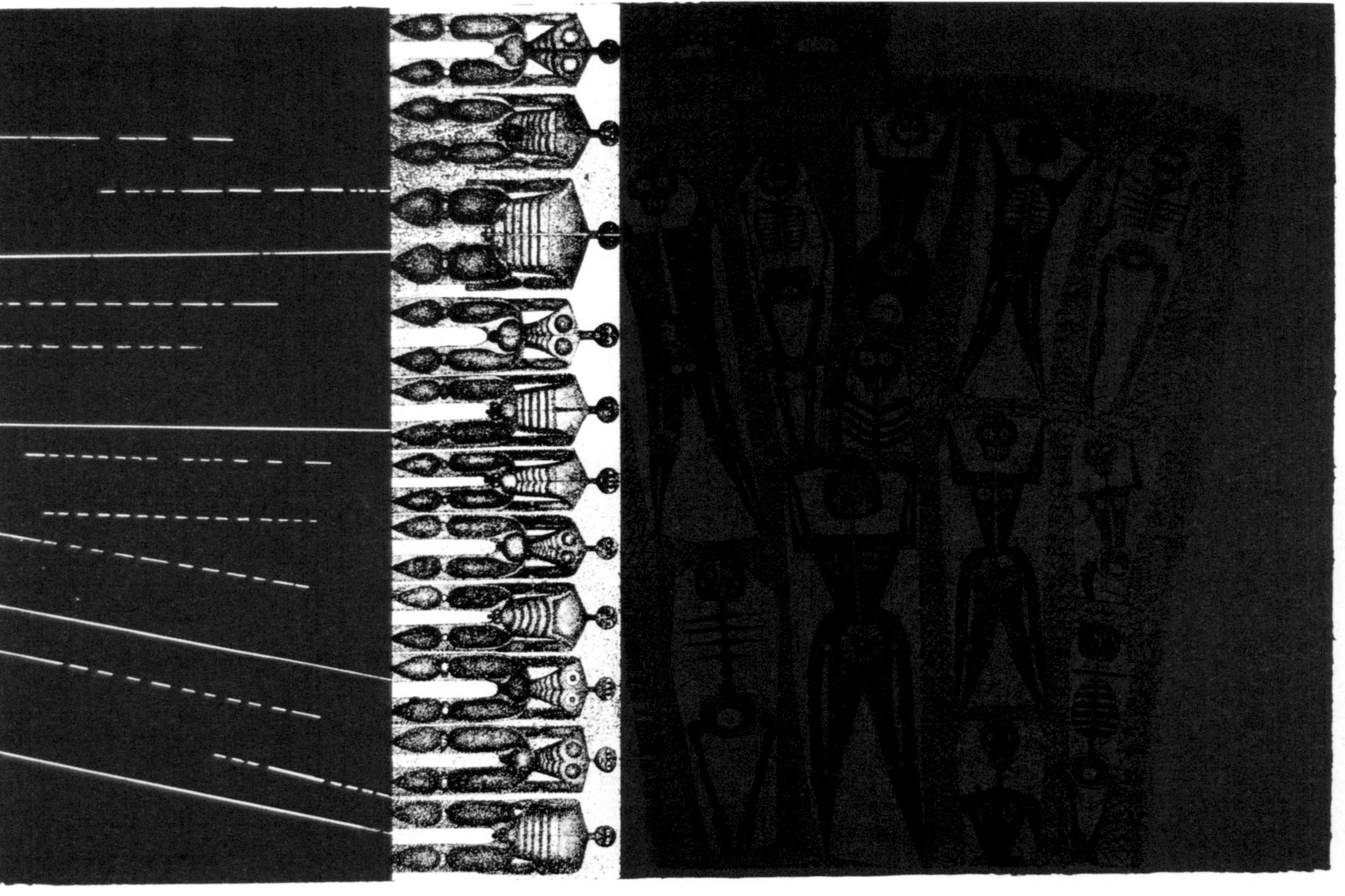

Margarita Pellegrin, Shooting, 1979, screen print, 76.1 × 53.4 cm, Kunstfonds, Staatliche Kunstsammlungen Dresden, inv. no. G 289/94

That's when I developed a critical attitude in general. Not towards the GDR, because I was very grateful and couldn't betray the country that had extended its hand to me. But towards the problems, privileges and corruption and many things that I not only found here, but that I also saw in Latin America.

The artist César Olhagaray on his life in the GDR, interview as part of the research project *Art in Networks—The GDR and its Global Relations*, see p. 171.

Trần Việt Sơn, illustration from *Golden Grave—Silver Grave/The Duckweed Queen* [two Vietnamese fairy tales], 1979, mezzotint lithograph, 34.9 × 19 cm, Kustodie der Hochschule für Bildende Künste Dresden, inv. no. B 2337

Võ Hồng
Chương-Đài

A New Socialist Order: The Prints of Trịnh Kim Vinh and Trần Việt Sơn

The Socialist Republic of Vietnam (North Vietnam) participated in many artistic exchanges with the German Democratic Republic (GDR) from the 1950s to the 1980s, sending artists both to undertake advanced studies and to serve as goodwill ambassadors between the two countries. The earliest such effort was in 1951 when a Vietnamese delegation of influential writers, poets, musicians, and artists attended the Third World Festival of Youth and Students in East Berlin; among them were the artists Nguyễn Đỗ Cung (1912–77) and Diệp Minh Châu (1919–2002). The former would soon become the founding director of the Hanoi Museum of Fine Arts, and its research arms, the Institute of Fine Arts, as well as *Fine Arts Magazine*. The latter would become the most influential sculptor of Vietnamese socialist realist monuments and statues. The Anti-French Resistance War had been waged since 1945, and artists, writers, and intellectuals played an important role in promoting cultural diplomacy abroad to garner political legitimacy and military support for the fight at home.

Though they supported the revolutionary cause, however, their march toward socialist realism did not necessarily devolve into a rigid prescription. While the content of artworks shifted from bourgeois portraits to paintings of manual workers, peasants, and armed forces, forms and styles continued to draw upon and transform an aesthetic synthesis of European modernism, pre-colonial material cultures, and modern movements in China and Japan. The first generation of socialist realist artists were the graduates of the École des Beaux-arts de l'Indochine (EBAI) in Hanoi, which was founded in 1924 by Victor Tardieu. The neoclassical French painter greatly admired the pre-colonial material cultures that he saw in the temples, pagodas, and villages. He also understood the commercial potential of training students who could create Orientalist works for the European bourgeois market. Tardieu hired masters in lacquer, metalwork, woodworking, and other specializations to teach their technical skills. During the anti-colonial war and thereafter, EBAI alumni promoted research about the cultural importance of these practices and experimentation with the processes and materials as a way to recover aesthetic genealogies that had been abolished or marginalized by the French. An important practice that received renewed attention was woodblock printing, notably three principal types: the Buddhist and Taoist scriptures from the 11th to 19th centuries, government documents from the Confucian dynasties, and folk prints from the 16th to 19th centuries.[1] Artists had been looking at these genealogies during their school days at EBAI, and they would revisit these sources with revolutionary vigor as inspiration for an anti-colonial and post-colonial modernism.

These woodblock printing practices offered a template for the socialist realist posters created to rally support for the revolution, as well as smaller lithograph prints such as those made by Trịnh Kim Vinh (1932–2018) and Trần Việt Sơn (1935–2009) during their advanced studies at the Hochschule für Bildende Künste Dresden (Dresden Academy of Fine Arts) in the 1970s. Vinh and Sơn[2] were among 83 Vietnamese artists sent abroad by the communist government between the late 1940s and the late 1980s.[3] The artists' leadership roles during

---

1   A Summary of Vietnam's History of Ancient Graphic Arts, in: Đồ Hoạ Cổ Việt Nam (The Ancient Graphic Arts of Vietnam), eds. Phan Cẩm Thượng, Lê Quốc Việt and Cung Khắc Lược, Hanoi 1999/2022, p. 30–36.
2   Vietnamese names are ordered surname followed by given names; hence, Trịnh Kim Vinh's surname is Trịnh, and her given names are Kim Vinh. After the first mention, the person is referred to by their given name.
3   Appendix G: List of Vietnamese artists who graduated from the Communist Bloc, in: Huỳnh Bội Trân, Vietnamese Aesthetics From 1925 Onwards, PhD dissertation, University of Sydney, 2018, p. 413–18.

Trịnh Kim Vinh, Coal Opencast Mining in Cẩm Phả, 1973, lithograph, 37.5 × 89.6cm, Kustodie der Hochschule für Bildende Künste Dresden, inv. no. B 2340

the war against France and later the Civil War between North Vietnam and the Republic of Vietnam (South Vietnam) gave them special status, allowing them to further their artistic practices in socialist bloc and non-aligned countries, and to rise in the administrative ranks.

Trịnh Kim Vinh (1932–2018)

Vinh was born in 1932 in Hanoi, and at age 13 joined the war against France, quickly becoming a leader in the Youth Union, head of a women's propaganda team, and other mobilizing units in the 1940s and early 1950s.[4] When the Việt Minh (League for the Independence of Vietnam)[5] moved their headquarters to the mountains of Việt Bắc, many EBAI alumni followed and reconstituted the School of Fine Arts with Tô Ngọc Vân as the founding director in 1950. The respected artist and intellectual saw talent in Vinh and encouraged her interest in the visual arts.[6] Perhaps because she had organized literacy campaigns, the Provisional Revolutionary Government sent her to China to study pedagogy from 1951 to 1953; upon her return to North Vietnam, she spent a decade working at primary and secondary schools as a teacher and administrator. Her trajectory shifted after she completed post-secondary studies at the Hanoi College of Fine Arts in 1969[7] and joined the Research Department. She took leave from 1970 to 1974 to pursue her postgraduate course at the Academy of Fine Arts in Dresden, where she focused on lithography with her teachers Gerhard Kettner and Friderun Bondzin.

The Albertinum Museum exhibition *Revolutionary Romances? Global Art Histories in the GDR* displays a series of prints that exemplify a meeting of pre-colonial Vietnamese graphic arts, the idyllic sensibility of Impressionism and Post-Impressionism, and the optimism of socialist realist graphic posters. Like other artists who fought in and supported the revolutionary forces, Vinh had created many works on paper that could be quickly executed using easily transported materials such as colored pencils, charcoal, and gouache. She also painted propaganda posters that could be reproduced with a limited color palette, featuring symbols and compositions made for a popular audience. In sharp contrast, Vinh's lithograph prints from her Dresden period are incredibly detailed, requiring concentrated time, machinery, and care. Vietnamese artists and cultural officials had waged extensive criticism and self-criticism sessions in the 1940s over the 'unrevolutionary' nature of practices that consumed much time and material, but de facto artists continued to work in media

---

4   Vân Thanh: Người phụ nữ tài hoa bên đời nhạc sỹ Lưu Hữu Phước (The Talented Woman in the Life of the Musician Lưu Hữu Phước): https://www.nguoiduatin.vn/nguoi-phu-nu-tai-hoa-ben-doi-nhac-sy-luu-huu-phuoc-a64709.html (accessed on: 29.3.2023). See also Trịnh Kim Vinh Biography: https://vietnamtheartofwar.com/1932/07/23/trinh-kim-vinh-biography/ (accessed on: 29.3.2023).

5   Việt Minh is short for Việt Nam Độc lập Đồng minh (League for the Independence of Vietnam); it was formed by the Indochinese Communist Party, the precursor to the Vietnamese Communist Party, to unite various factions for the First Indochina War against the French. See Christopher Goscha: Vietnam: A New History, New York 2016.

6   See Thanh (note 4).

7   Trường Đại Học Mỹ Thuật, Hà Nội, 1925-1990 (The School of Fine Arts, Hanoi: 1925–1990), Hanoi 1990, p. 200.

that demanded attention and resources. What changed was the prominence of certain aesthetic references and alignments, and one of them was the centuries-old woodblock print that was ubiquitous in both secular and religious life. Vinh's lithography training accorded with both that lineage and the more recent socialist realist poster.

Created in 1972 and 1973, Vinh's prints present a tranquil world that celebrates work and camaraderie, notably women's labor. A female guerrilla enjoys a quiet moment against a somewhat abstracted landscape (p. 116); women and men reap a bountiful harvest; male and female soldiers travel in pairs through the forest or down a river; children walk unhurriedly in pairs with their books and sacks. A riverine composition transforms a coal mining site into an undulating passage between the sea and the cut terraces while a group of workers steadily maneuver a giant ladle pouring molten iron into molds. These prints possess an air of intimacy subtly created with close-up portraits and repetitions of shapes and gestures that invite the viewer into the scene and move us through its rhythms.

The bright yellows and swirling backdrops are reminiscent of Impressionism, Post-Impressionism, and Expressionism, such as the portraits and rural landscapes of Vincent Van Gogh, Camille Pissarro, and Edvard Munch. The image of the female guerrilla (p. 116) evokes Van Gogh's *Sunflowers* (1888–89) both in the brush-like texture and in the shape of the plant on the left side of the composition. The peasant woman wearing a rifle was a typical wartime image used to depict popular support for the revolution. Her cherubic face transports the romanticism of Pierre Auguste Renoir's Parisian bourgeois picnickers to the North Vietnamese countryside, revealing the deftness of artists trained in European modernism to create a new movement called Vietnamese socialist realism.

Vinh's personages bewitch us with a calm that comes from abundance and confidence—in this case, symbolically an affirmation of socialist economic planning and communist political leadership. This vision of balance and harmony extends to regions populated by ethnic minorities. During the war years, many artists lived and worked with guerrilla units in the northern mountains and central highlands of Vietnam, regions with many different ethnic groups that were exploited both during colonialism by the French and during the Civil War by the majority Kinh or Việt ethnic group. People from minority ethnic groups became common subjects for artists, who were mainly Kinh—reflecting both the artists' admiration and exoticization of the communities and the government's propaganda of a unified front against foreign aggressors.

After she finished her studies in Dresden in 1974, Vinh returned to Hanoi as Head of the Drawing Department at the College of Fine Arts in Hanoi. In the post-1975 aftermath of the Civil War, the Hanoi government sent administrators to take over the institutions of the former South Vietnam. Vinh was a part of that wave, becoming Head of the Department of Plastic and Graphic Arts and Vice Rector of the newly named Ho Chi Minh City College of Fine Arts, formerly the Saigon National College of Fine Arts, for three decades until her retirement in 2009.[8]

Trần Việt Sơn (1935–2009)

A year after Vinh's departure from Dresden, Trần Việt Sơn went to Leipzig to learn German in anticipation of his advanced studies in fine arts. Born in 1935 in the Quảng Bình province of the French protectorate of Annam, his given name was Trần Thăng Giai. In the mid-1950s, he joined the Anti-French Resistance War. He then studied art at the Hanoi College of Fine Arts in 1958, at the All-Ukrainian Art Institute in Kyiv in the Soviet Union from 1961 to 1964, and again in Hanoi from 1964 to 1966, at the Faculty of Silk Painting and Wood

8   Thái Nguyên: Nhà giáo, họa sĩ Trịnh Kim Vinh: Sức sáng tạo nghệ thuật mạnh mẽ (Teacher and artist Trinh Kim Vinh: great artistic creativity): https://thainguyentv.vn/nha-giao-hoa-si-trinh-kim-vinh-suc-sang-tao-nghe-thuat-manh-me-13000.html (accessed on: 29.3.2023).

Engraving. During the Civil War he worked as a battlefield painter. Sơn left for East Germany in 1975, first to learn German at the Herder-Institut in Leipzig and then to undertake his postgraduate degree with Gerhard Kettner at the Academy of Fine arts in Dresden. He graduated with a solo exhibition at the academy in 1979. He would serve at the Hanoi University of Fine Arts as a lecturer, as Vice President of the Graphic Arts Faculty, and as Vice Director. Significantly, he also served as Director of the Institute of Fine Arts and as Director of the Fine Arts Department of the Ministry of Culture in Vietnam.[9]

During his time in Dresden, he produced two artist books and many lithograph prints that show a clear affiliation with the centuries-old woodblock prints found in North Vietnam. While Vinh's prints suggest an affinity with the long history of woodblock printing in Vietnam, Sơn's prints directly adapt much of the style and content found in the folk and religious prints. The images in his 1979 children's book *Binh und der Mondkuchen* (Binh and the Moon Cake) are remarkably akin to those from Đông Hồ, a northern Vietnamese village renown for its folk woodblock art since the 16th century. Sơn's appropriation of this tradition is fitting for a book about the autumn moon festival—given the popularity of Đông Hồ depictions of zodiac cycles and festival greetings. Families and villages would celebrate the annual end of the harvest season with mooncakes and paper lanterns. Sơn's front book cover shows a boy dressed in a communist school uniform with the red neckerchief, wearing a dragon head and holding in his right hand a plate with a mooncake and in his left hand a star-shaped paper toy with an image of Vietnam. The book's back cover shows a paper lantern, two stylized clouds, and four toys in the shape of fishes, a symbol of fertility. Folk prints commonly depict children carrying small animals such as poultry and tortoises as symbolic representations of bounty and the harmonious coexistence of humans and non-humans.[10] A Vietnamese viewer would understand Sơn's use of this symbolic order to propagate the idea of a Vietnam unified in body and spirit by the Communist Party and well positioned for a future of prosperity.

His proficiency with traditional Vietnamese prints can also be seen in the images he created in 1979 for his storybook with the two Vietnamese fairy tales *Goldenes Grab, Silbernes Grab* (Golden Grave, Silver Grave) and *Die Wasserlinsenkönigin* (The Duckweed Queen). The first is about an impoverished girl who beseeches Buddha to save the rice crop so that her family may have food. The direct references are religious prints that date back to at least the 11th century and generally depict the personages by rank and size from top to bottom. The viewer would readily identify Buddha, who would be largest figure illuminated by a halo, if not the central figure, in the top half of the composition. The composition order would continue downward with representations of Bodhisattvas and civil officials, generals, and other high-status personages.[11] It was rare to see depictions of common folk such as peasants. Sơn's image of a poor girl petitioning Buddha for benevolence is unusual not

9   Trần Việt Sơn Biography: https://vietnamtheartofwar.com/1935/03/31/tran-viet-son-tran-thang-giai-biography/ (accessed on: 6.6.2023).
10   Patterns and Concepts, in: Đồ Hoạ Cổ Việt Nam (The Ancient Graphic Arts of Vietnam), eds. Phan Cẩm Thượng, Lê Quốc Việt, Cung Khắc Lược, Hanoi 1999/2022, p. 84–86.
11   Ibid., p. 87–88.

only in its subject matter but also in the closeness of the human and the sacred, with no intermediary figures. He has reduced the composition to the two main characters, with Buddha enshrouded in an aura of radiating light and stylized clouds. This storyline is peculiar, given the communist prohibition of religion as an "opium of the masses". But it may be that Sơn's borrowing of a centuries-long Vietnamese tradition allowed him to carve out space for representing religious figures. Moreover, his portrayal of the peasant inserts a figure of communist value into a historically hierarchical and exclusive genre.

Trần Việt Sơn and Trịnh Kim Vinh were among a generation of artists initially trained in European modernism, whose practices would be transformed by their experiences as war-time painters and their reevaluation of Vietnamese material cultures and pre-colonial practices for the construction of socialist modernism. Their advanced studies at the Academy of Fine Arts in Dresden allowed them time and space away from the war front and domestic politics to study lithography, which they infused with subjects and styles from North Vietnam. The prints they made during their Dresden period complicate easy divisions between the modern and the traditional or West European modernism and socialist realism and instead propose reinvigorated aesthetics and a vision of a new socialist order.

Trần Việt Sơn, cover design for the children's book *Binh und der Mondkuchen* (Binh and the Moon Cake) by Renate Lange, ed. Verlag Junge Welt Berlin, 1982, offset, 27.7×40 cm, Kustodie der Hochschule für Bildende Künste Dresden, inv. no. B 2339

Trịnh Kim Vinh at *INTERGRAFIK 73*, Berlin,
Altes Museum, 1973

Guillermo Deisler, **The Child's Name Is Today, not Tomorrow**, 1970s, postcard, screen print, 15.6 × 11 cm, Kupferstich-Kabinett, Staatliche Kunstsammlungen Dresden, inv. no. B 1979–15/79

Dieter Wuttge, Solidarity—Now More Than Ever, 1975, lithograph, linocut, 57 × 45 cm, Kunstfonds, Staatliche Kunstsammlungen Dresden, inv. no. L 04528

Rudolf Bergander, Therese from Togo, 1963, oil on canvas, 81.5 × 71 cm,
Albertinum, Staatliche Kunstsammlungen Dresden, inv. no. 79/43

The time in the GDR has had a great impact on me so far and was a great inspiration—not only in terms of methodology and the graphic work with its view on the world, but above all the relationships with other countries were very important to me. To Mexican art, to revolutionary art. I needed these impressions in my country as a member of the Palestinian minority.

The artist Abed Abdi on his time as a student in the GDR in the 1960s, interview as part of the research project *Art in Networks—The GDR and its Global Relations*, see p. 171.

INTERGRAFIK 73, Berlin, Altes Museum, 1973.
photo: Hans-Jürgen May

Annabel
Ruckdeschel

The International Graphic Arts Triennial *INTERGRAFIK* (1965–1990) and the Limits of Transcontinental Solidarity in the GDR

Large international exhibitions such as *documenta*, which has been held in Kassel every five years since 1955, relate the place of the exhibition and the host country organizing it to the (art) world. The German Democratic Republic (GDR) also pursued that intention with the exhibition *INTERGRAFIK*. It was an international triennial for the graphic arts and was held in East Berlin from 1965 to 1990. It sought to present a relationship to international art that was very different from that presented in Kassel. Already for its very first exhibition, proposal papers and newspaper articles in the GDR assessed *INTERGRAFIK* as an alternative to *documenta*. Klaus Weidner wrote in the newspaper *Neues Deutschland*: "'Intergrafik 65' is no 'international art show.' It could not and did not intend to be that. The immoderate self-overestimation of representing 'the art of the twentieth century' with a few hundred abstract paintings can be left to the organizers of *documenta*, say, and other monster shows. But artists have come together in the exhibition who have something to say to the world, more than all the different 'model cases' of world art that become talking points in West Germany and other countries."[1]

What Weidner and others saw as the commonality and message of *INTERGRAFIK* to the world was a profession of peace, friendship, and anti-imperialist solidarity—concepts that were ideologically charged during the Cold War and associated with an anti-Western rhetoric. This exhibition of graphic art sought to bring together positions against exploitative capitalism and Western imperialism. It is notable that it combined works of arts and artists from both sides of the Iron Curtain as well as from nonaligned countries and thus sought to be a "collection of progressive, humanistically inclined artists working in the realist spirit."[2]

An International "Galerie auf Zeit"

In addition to the Deutsche Kunstausstellung (German Art Exhibition) held in Dresden since 1946,[3] *INTERGRAFIK* and the *Biennale der Ostseeländer* (Biennial of Baltic Sea Countries), organized in Rostock since 1965, were among the central periodic art exhibitions of the GDR.[4] The art critic Lothar Lang characterized *INTERGRAFIK* as a "Galerie auf Zeit" (temporary gallery),[5] which alluded to Arnold Bode's vision of *documenta* as a "museum of 100 days" and thus underscored the claim that it was a show of museum quality. *INTERGRAFIK* was organized by the central executive committee of the Verband Bildender Künstler der DDR (VBK; Association of Visual Artists of the GDR).[6] The exhibition was

---

1   Klaus Weidner: Künstler bekennen sich zum Leben, in: Neues Deutschland, supplement no. 27, April 3, 1965, p. 2.
2   Konzeptpapier Intergrafik 73 (concept for Intergrafik 73), AdK Berlin, VBK-Zentralvorstand 1367.
3   In 1946, the (first) *Allgemeine Deutsche Kunstausstellung* (General German Art Exhibition) was shown in Dresden. The exhibitions from 1949 to 1968/69 (II–VI) were called *Deutsche Kunstausstellung* (German Art Exhibition), and, finally, from the seventh exhibition in 1972/73 the name was *Kunstausstellung der DDR* (Art Exhibition of the GDR).
4   See Elke Neumann, Die Biennale der Ostseeländer: Außen- und kulturpolitische Dimensionen der größten Internationalen Kunstausstellung der DDR, PhD thesis. Technische Universität Berlin, 2022.
5   Lothar Lang: Zur Intergrafik 1980, in: Die Weltbühne 35 (1980), issue no. 10, p. 313–14, here p. 313.
6   Founded in 1950 as the Verband Bildender Künstler Deutschlands (Association of Visual Artists of Germany), it was renamed Verband Bildender Künstler der DDR (Association of Visual Artists of the GDR) in 1970.

initiated in 1965 by the president of the Association, Lea Grundig, and by the artists Ronald Paris and Arno Mohr.[7] Originally, it was supposed to adopt the concept of the exhibition *Zeitgenössische Deutsche Grafik* (Contemporary German Graphic Art) presented in East Berlin in 1955 and offer a survey of the graphic art of the GDR, but Lea Grundig advocated that the program should be international and that artists from the "capitalist West" should be invited in order to create a broad alliance with the "progressive forces" of those countries. Graphic art was particularly well supported in the GDR because its reproducibility and ability to be disseminated made it seemed suited to underscoring the non-elitist claim of art. Moreover, it was easier and less expensive to transport graphic works international than sculptures or paintings, which surely benefited the focus of an international exhibition in the GDR on this medium. Already in the year of its founding, efforts were being made to repeat *INTERGRAFIK* as a triennial. The Artists' Union of the USSR supported this plan, and so in the future (with three exceptions), the exhibition was held at three-year intervals.[8]

The international agenda of *INTERGRAFIK* was evident not only in the policy of inviting artists but also in the choice of hosting sites. The very first of these ambitious large-scale exhibitions brought together 420 artists from twenty-one countries. With *INTERGRAFIK*, the VBK was pursuing its goal of constantly building up its international networks. The number of countries from which the exhibitors came almost doubled from twenty-one in 1965 to thirty-nine in 1967 and then increased almost continuously to seventy-eight in 1987. Only the final show, which opened five months after the fall of the Berlin Wall, clearly reduced the number of countries represented to sixty. The main exhibition sites of *INTER-GRAFIK* were located in what was then the center of East Berlin The denomination "Berlin, capital of the GDR" in the catalogs reflects the ongoing conflict over the status of the divided Berlin and the attitude of the GDR in insisting on this description not recognized by the Federal Republic of Germany. The first exhibition was held in the spaces of the Nationalgalerie as well as the Neue Berliner Galerie im Marstall. In 1967, *INTERGRAFIK* moved into the Altes Museum. The triennial of graphic art remained there up to and including 1973. After a brief use of spaces in the Museum für Deutsche Geschichte im Zeughaus, it moved to the Ausstellungszentrum am Fernsehturm (Exhibition Center at the Berlin Television Tower). The initiative to send *INTERGRAFIK* as a traveling exhibition to selected participating countries was never solidified. Only *INTERGRAFIK 67* traveled to Oslo after opening in East Berlin as well as to venues in several Eastern European countries: Leningrad, Karlovy Vary, Warsaw, and Budapest.

The triennial format per se testifies to the ambitions of the GDR that *INTERGRAFIK* should bring it recognition on the stage of large international exhibitions. The *INTER-GRAFIK* triennial and the *Biennale der Ostseeländer* were the GDR's contributions to the phenomenon that Anthony Gardner and Charles Green have described as the "second wave" of international biennials.[9] Following successful large exhibitions such as the Venice Biennale, founded in 1895, biennials and triennials were established outside of Western centers from the 1950s to the 1970s. For example, they include the Bienal de São Paulo (founded in 1951), the Ljubljana Biennale of Graphic Arts (founded in 1955), and the Bienal de La Habana (founded in 1984). The socialist countries of Eastern Europe also contributed to these new foundations with, for example, the International Print Triennial in Kraków (founded in 1966) and the Tallin Print Triennial (founded in 1968).[10] The VBK emphasized,

---

7   See Karlen Vesper: Ronald Paris: Wahr und wahrhaftig, Berlin, 2012, p. 202.

8   Nine *INTERGRAFIK* exhibitions were held in all: in 1965, 1967, 1970, 1973, 1976, 1980, 1984, 1987, and 1990. On the support from the Artists' Union of the USSR, see "INTERGRAFIK 65 gewürdigt," in: Neues Deutschland, July 1, 1965, p. 4.

9   Anthony Gardner and Charles Green: Biennials, Triennials, and documenta: The Exhibitions That Created Contemporary Art, Chichester, West Sussex 2016.

10 See Beata Hock: Curator's Trade in Ideals: Exhibitions, Exhibition History, and Networks of Artistic Solidarity in Cold War Times, in: Curating (Post-)Socialist Environments, eds. Philipp Schorch, Daniel Habit, Bielefeld, 2021, p. 185–206; Wiktor Komorowski: Cold War Exhibitions of Graphic Art: Tallinn Print Triennial (1968) and the Reversed Power of Printed Image, lecture at the conference *Art Exhibitions as Intersections in Post War Europe*, Stockholm, May 11–12, 2021.

however, that in its function of uniting realism-minded artists *INTERGRAFIK* "differed fundamentally from the biennials and triennials of capitalist countries but also [from] similar international events in several socialist countries such as the People's Republic of Poland, the ČSSR, and the SFRJ. These international exhibitions of graphic art organized by the aforementioned socialist counties are essentially based on antisocialist conceptions of connecting to so-called world art (West art), which for years has been dominated by the primacy of different varieties of 'abstract' art. Works of Socialist Realism are the exception."[11]

The Cultural and Foreign Policy Framework

A large-scale international show such as *INTERGRAFIK* was possible in the GDR only within the framework of official cultural and foreign policy, which organized and regulated the artistic exchange and the contact across national borders. The principles of the international show were coupled to longer lines in the development of the country's cultural and foreign policies. The essential leitmotifs of "peace", "friendship", and "anti-imperialist solidarity" were brought to bear but weighted different proposal papers and the presentation of the large exhibition to others. In the beginning, the accompanying texts were dominated by the ideas of "peace" and "antifascism." From the time of its founding, the GDR stylized itself as an antifascist country of peace in opposition to the FRG which was striving to rearm. At the same time, GDR foreign policy in the mid-1960s profited from a reduction in tension that made gradual political rapprochement seem possible.[12]

Frank Ruddigkeit, exhibition poster *INTERGRAFIK 73*, offset, 115 × 81 cm, Deutsches Historisches Museum, inv. no. P 98/75, 98000371

From the 1970s onward, *INTERGRAFIK* placed greater emphasis on "anti-imperial solidarity." This was a consequence of the foreign cultural policy of the late 1960s and early 1970s, which was striving to create broad international alliances, especially with countries of the Global South.[13] Building international relationships was necessary because ever since its founding the GDR had been struggling for recognition under international law and was not diplomatically recognized by many, primarily Western countries.[14] In the field of culture, at least, the triennial of graphic art helped it get around the West's policy of refusing to recognize it, which is why Gregor Lersch has described it as part of a far-ranging "crypto-diplomacy" of the GDR.[15] That situation changed, however, with West Germany's new Eastern policy under Willy Brandt. The Federal Republic of Germany and

11 Vorlage an das ZK des VBK, betrifft das Konzept der Intergrafik 70 (submission to the Central Committee of the Artists' Association, concerns the concept of Intergrafik 70), October 30, 1969, AdK Berlin, VBK-Zentralvorstand 1370.
12 See Michael Lemke: Die Außenbeziehungen der DDR (1949–1966). Prinzipien, Grundlagen, Zäsuren und Handlungsspielräume, in: Die DDR und der Westen. Transnationale Beziehungen, 1949–1989, ed. Ulrich Pfeil, Berlin 2001, p. 63–80.
13 Christian Saehrendt: Kunst im Kampf für das "Sozialistisches Weltsystem". Auswärtige Kulturpolitik der DDR in Afrika und Nahost, Stuttgart 2017.
14 The Hallstein doctrine promulgated by the Federal Republic of Germany judged diplomatic relationships of third countries with the GDR to be an "unfriendly act."
15 Gregor H. Lersch: Art From East Germany? Die internationale Verflechtung der Kunst in der DDR: Ausstellung, Rezeption im Ausland, Frankfurt (Oder) 2021, p. 123.

the German Democratic Republic signed the Basic Treaty on December 21, 1972.[16] This was followed by both countries being admitted to the United Nations as well as international recognition of the GDR by numerous countries. That also had an effect on *INTERGRAFIK* in that a growing number of countries participated. *INTERGRAFIK 73*, which opened between the ratification of the Basic Treaty on June 13 and the GDR's admittance to the United Nations on September 18, 1973, represented a symbolic high point in this respect. Moreover, it was part of the program of the lavishly planned X. World Festival of Youth and Students, held in Berlin in the summer of 1973 under the motto "For peace, friendship, and anti-imperialist solidarity." The exhibition, which profited from exchange with international delegations, was therefore presented as an international meeting place for young artists.

INTERGRAFIK grew in this period above all thanks to the increasing participation of African, Asian, and Latin American countries. The exhibition thus reflected the efforts of the GDR to improve diplomatic relationships with these countries, some of which had become independent in the decolonization process and thus achieve a breakthrough in recognition policy.[17] Another goal was to win over for real socialism nations that were active in the nonaligned movement and seeking a way out of the bipolarity of the East-West conflict in the Cold War. Of the forty-eight countries and groups that *INTERGRAFIK 73* claimed to represent, for example, fifteen were taking part for the first time that year.[18] They included Bangladesh, Algeria, the Laotian Patriotic Front, the Syrian Arab Republic, Tunisia, Oman and the Persian Gulf region, Kuwait, the United Republic of Tanzania, the People's Republic of Yemen, South Africa, and the Palestinian Liberation Organization (PLO). For *INTER-GRAFIK 73* in particular, the VBK tried to highlight anti-imperialist policy as a shared concern and to place related themes and motifs: "the accusations against the imperialism of the USA; solidarity with the peoples of Vietnam, Laos, and Cambodia; solidarity with the struggle of the Arab peoples; [...] accusations against the policy of racism in America and South Africa; solidarity with the wars of liberation in these countries; [...] declarations of alliance and solidarity with the revolution in Cuba and Chile."[19]

The central executive committee of the VBK was responsible for planning and executing of *INTERGRAFIK*. Its proposal papers and reports were agreed on with the Zentralkomitee (ZK) of the Sozialistische Einheitspartei (SED; Socialist Unity Party), and in particular its cultural section. When laying out political and artistic baselines for international cooperation as well, the VBK worked with the Ministry of Culture. The latter was supposed to inform the minister of culture of the socialist countries about the guiding ideas for *INTERGRAFIK* "with the goal of encourage active state influence on the selection of works to ensure the exhibition's core of Socialist Realism."[20] The VBK worked with the Foreign Ministry to influence submissions from nonsocialist countries. Together with the Liga für Völkerfreundschaft (International Friendship League), the aforementioned authorities were responsible for winning over artists from abroad. In 1973, *INTERGRAFIK* also worked with the Freie Deutsche Jugend (FDJ; Free German Youth). That makes it clear that efforts were already being made in the runup to the exhibition to encourage international networking, on the one hand, and, on the other, to defuse as much as possible any conflicts that could result from international exchange.

16   This treaty regulated relationships between the two Germany states. It meant that the FRG recognized the GDR under constitutional law but not under international law. See Jens Hacker: Grundlagenvertrag, in: Handbuch zur deutschen Einheit, 1949–1989–1999, eds. Werner Weidenfeld, Karl-Rudolf Korte, Bonn 1999, p. 417–430.

17   See Lemke 2001 (note 12), p. 78; Saehrendt 2017 (note 13).

18   I have chosen this formulation because, especially in the case of the nonsocialist countries, these were not official submissions but rather the individual progressive artists with whom *INTERGRAFIK* was cooperating; nevertheless, the name of the nation is listed in the catalog. This was the case, for example with the Western European countries and the USA but also with South Africa (a contribution from the African National Congress was shown).

19   Bericht VBK-DDR, X. Weltfestspiele der Jugend und Studenten (report from Artists' Association of the GDR, X. World Festival of Youth and Students), AdK Berlin, VBK-Zentralvorstand 1378.

20   Konzept zur Intergrafik 73 (concept for Intergrafik 73), AdK Berlin, VBK-Zentralvorstand 1367.

Djordje Zivkovic, Man an his City, etching, 48 × 37 cm

This strategy is also reflected in the process of selecting works. Although until 1987 *INTERGRAFIK* boasted of having no jury and projected an image of openness to the outside world.[21] In truth, however, the organization of the exhibition was based on a calculated policy of invitation. The submissions from the socialist fraternal states were organized independently by the corresponding artist association and were thus subject to its control. Groups of leftist artists from the West were targeted for invitation and their contributions approved in advance. The meetings of artists in preparation for *INTERGRAFIK* were also subject to this idea of control. For example, as part of the *VII. Kunstausstellung der DDR* (VII. Art Exhibition of the GDR) in Dresden in 1972–73, there were meetings in which representatives of the countries participating in *INTERGRAFIK* were to be "advised" on its objectives. These included conversations among artists and cultural functionaries from Chile, Uruguay, Mexico, Columbia, Argentina, India, Sri Lanka, Nepal, Peru, Japan, the USA, and Indonesia.[22]

Imagining Transcontinental Solidarity

INTERGRAFIK presented an idealized relationship of the GDR to the world, imagining broad alliances of solidarity across national borders and continents.[23] It therefore tried to produce an image of political and aesthetic unity within diversity. Despite the invitation policy described above, works were also submitted and exhibited that were, as a report from 1976 puts it, "intentionally or unintentionally, politically ambiguous" or "formalist games."[24] The VBK permitted a certain artistic range in order to be able to emphasize aesthetic diversity to the outside world. For example, *INTERGRAFIK* includes works, such as the contributions from nonaligned Yugoslavia in 1973, that were far from representational. In 1976, according to an internal analysis, around five percent of the works shown were abstract. At the same time, the VBK sought to limit the stylistic spectrum to varieties of figural realism. From 1965 onward, it was already emphasizing the challenge of "securing and expanding the Socialist Realist core with all determination while retaining the necessary breadth of the alliance with all anti-imperialist forces."[25]

By demonstrating alliances of solidarity across the globe in the medium of graphic art, the VBK was trying to counter a constant risk of the international contributions become to heterogeneous. An important role here was played by works of art that referred to proxy conflicts in the Cold War in which the GDR was positioning itself politically. On the one hand, the triennial showed contributions by socialist parties involved in conflicts; on the other, artistic declarations of solidarity with them. In the 1960s, contributions from the Democratic Republic of Vietnam received particular attention. A solidarity bazaar that was a regular feature of every *INTERGRAFIK* was held in 1967 under the motto "Help the children of Vietnam." Works such as Gerhard Bondzin's *Vietnamese Mother* (p. 80) resulted from

21 In 1987, *INTERGRAFIK* reached the limits of its capacity and set up an international jury for the first time, which selected 512 artists from 1206.
22 See AdK Berlin, VBK-Zentralvorstand 1373.
23 I follow here the description of European activists' imagined connections to the anti-imperialist movements of the "Third World" as "imagined solidarities", in: Robert Gildea, James Mark, Niek Pas: European Radicals and the 'Third World'. Imagined Solidarities and Radical Networks, 1958–73, in: Cultural and Social History 8 (2011), issue no. 4, pp. 449–472.
24 Analyse der Intergrafik 76 (analysis of Intergrafik 76), AdK Berlin, VBK-Zentralvorstand 1385.
25 Vorlage an das Sekretariat des ZK, verf. durch VBK (submission to the secretariat of the Central Committee of the SED, drafted by the Artists' Association), October 10, 1969: "Konzeption für die Durchführung der internationalen Kunstausstellung 'Intergrafik' 1970 in Berlin," AdK Berlin, VBK-Zentralvorstand 1367. There had been a similar discussion in 1965 during a party group meeting on *INTERGRAFIK*, AdK Berlin, VBK-Zentralvorstand 1338.

Cover page of the magazine *Bildende Kunst*, 1977, no. 1, Pablo Neruda Brigade (Chile), Tribute to Pablo Neruda, series of 8 color lithographs, 1975, sheet 1

Elizabeth Catlett, There is a Woman in Every Color, 1975, color linoleum cut, screenprint, and woodcut on Arches paper, 56.52 cm × 76.04 cm, Bowdoin College Museum of Art, Brunswick, Maine, Museum Purchase, Lloyd O. and Marjorie Strong Coulter Fund, BCMA Accession#: 2015.61

deliberate encouragement of such propagandistic subjects. Artists in the GDR were already determined in the runup to the submission "that in addition to criticizing the American aggression in Vietnam and declaring solidarity with the Vietnamese people, in addition to antiwar themes and the call for peace, the GDR contribution in particular must make the national problems in Germany, the struggle against West German Imperialism and neofascism but also the peaceful building of socialism in the German Democratic Republic the main subjects of our collection."[26] The condemnation of the military coup in Chile in 1973 and the bloody end of the regime of Salvador Allende were other themes that the VBK prominently emphasized for the triennial of graphic art.

In collaboration with the artists Pedro Hernandez and Victor (Tapia) Contreras, a contribution by Chilean exiles was organized for *INTERGRAFIK 1976*, including the series *Tribute to Pablo Neruda*, whose title page was illustrated on the cover of the journal *Bildende Kunst*. *INTERGRAFIK* also tried to win over American artists critical of racism in the USA and active in the Black Arts Movement. For example, the exhibition repeatedly presented works by, among others, Charles White and Elizabeth Catlett, who had immigrated from the USA to Mexico in 1949. Catlett's *There Is a Woman in Every Color* is a reaction to the intersectionality of racism and sexism. The artist was awarded the *INTERGRAFIK* prize. With an eye to German history, however, it should be emphasized that the programmatic anti-imperialism of *INTERGRAFIK* also offered a stage to anti-Zionist messages. In a declaration of solidarity during the X. World Festival of Youth and Students, the chairman of the artists' association of the PLO, Ismail Shammout, and the president of the Akademie der Künste der DDR, Konrad Wolf, designed a poster that was exhibited at *INTERGRAFIK*. It reads "Long live the international solidarity against imperialism and Zionism." The political background for this was the signing of an official agreement between the SED and the PLO during the X. World Festival of Youth and Students, to which Yasser Arafat had been invited as guest of honor.

In light of this coming together of different political positions under the banner of "anti-imperialist solidarity," the question arises of the limits of imagining transcontinental networks. In the events flanking the exhibition, the VBK was trying to present a picture of the global struggle. There was no room to articulate contradiction or even friction between the various international actors, and even the VBK's internal reports present a smoothed-out picture. Where contradiction did occur during the meeting of international artists, it was passed over, as in the case of the Danish artist Dea Trier Mørch, who criticized the objectifying

---

26   Letter by Horst Weiß to Bezirksvorstand VBKD Halle (district board of the city of Halle of the Association of Visual Artists of the GDR), January 4, 1967, AdK Berlin, VBK Bezirksverband Halle 10.

representation of women at *INTERGRAFIK* in 1976.[27] It is reasonable to assume that several international artists who exhibited their works at *INTER-GRAFIK* had different expectations of the event and other ideas of transcontinental solidarity, and future research should try to reconstruct this.

Another limit on the imagining transcontinental alliances of solidarity was internal to the GDR. Again and again, the VBK reports noted discontent with the GDR contribution to *INTERGRAFIK*. They argued, according to the final report on *INTERGRAFIK 73*, that the themes of internationalism and international solidarity had been presented too weakly and had to be encouraged more.[28] Apparently, the effort to establish internationalist themes in domestic support of the arts did not live up to expectations. Hope was expressed in the summer 1973: "The immediate emotional experience of thousands of demonstrations of solidarity during the Weltfestspiele cannot yet be appreciated enough. That is also demonstrated by the many spontaneous drawings on the wall provided for that purpose in INTER-GRAFIK. A large number of artists depicted the immediate, deeply moving experience in sketches, some of which are outstanding."[29] One of these spontaneous drawings was *International Solidarity* by Ronald Paris. It shows people from a variety of backgrounds carrying banners with the words "peace" and "solidarity" in Latin, German, and Russian. Visitors to *INTERGRAFIK* were urged to immortalize themselves by writing their own individual messages of solidarity and sign this drawing. Their internationality presented turned out to be an unfulfilled program: Only eleven of the people who signed the sheet were from Western countries; nine were from countries of the Soviet Union; but most were from the GDR. The traces of the visitors on the sheet were disproportionate to the global vision in Paris's drawing. The work is less evidence of truly existing, transnational relationships than it is an idealized wish.

INTERGRAFIK lay the groundwork for the GDR's goals in cultural diplomacy and put its national work in the graphic arts in an imagined relationship to the world. It initiated artistic exchange and contact at the boundaries of socialist cultural and foreign policy between East and West, North and South, in the Cold War era. The theme of anti-imperialist solidarity was supposed to expand concrete international relationships in the field of art, expand the circle of international addressees, and make visible transcontinental exchange of socialist-minded artists. With regard to politics and aesthetics, *INTERGRAFIK* was thus operating within the tension between the strictly staked-out framework of possibilities of international exchange and the GDR's geographically broad ambitions for cultural diplomacy.

27 This occurred during the symposium *Politische Grafik und moderne Medien* (Political Graphic Art and Modern Media) of the VBK-DDR on November 8 and 9, 1976, in Berlin.

28 Bericht VBK-DDR, X. Weltfestspiele der Jugend und Studenten (report from Artists' Association of the GDR, X. World Festival of Youth and Students), AdK Berlin, VBK-Zentralvorstand 1378.

29 Ibid.

Ronald Paris, International Solidarity, 1973, graphite, 60.3 × 80.3 cm,
Kupferstich-Kabinett, Staatliche Kunstsammlungen Dresden, inv. no. C 1974-26

Paul Pedak, Sunshine for Whites and Sunshine for Blacks, sheet 1 from the series *To the Children of Soweto*, 1978, woodcut, 75.5 × 54.8 cm, Kunstfonds, Staatliche Kunstsammlungen Dresden, inv. no. 25/1/78

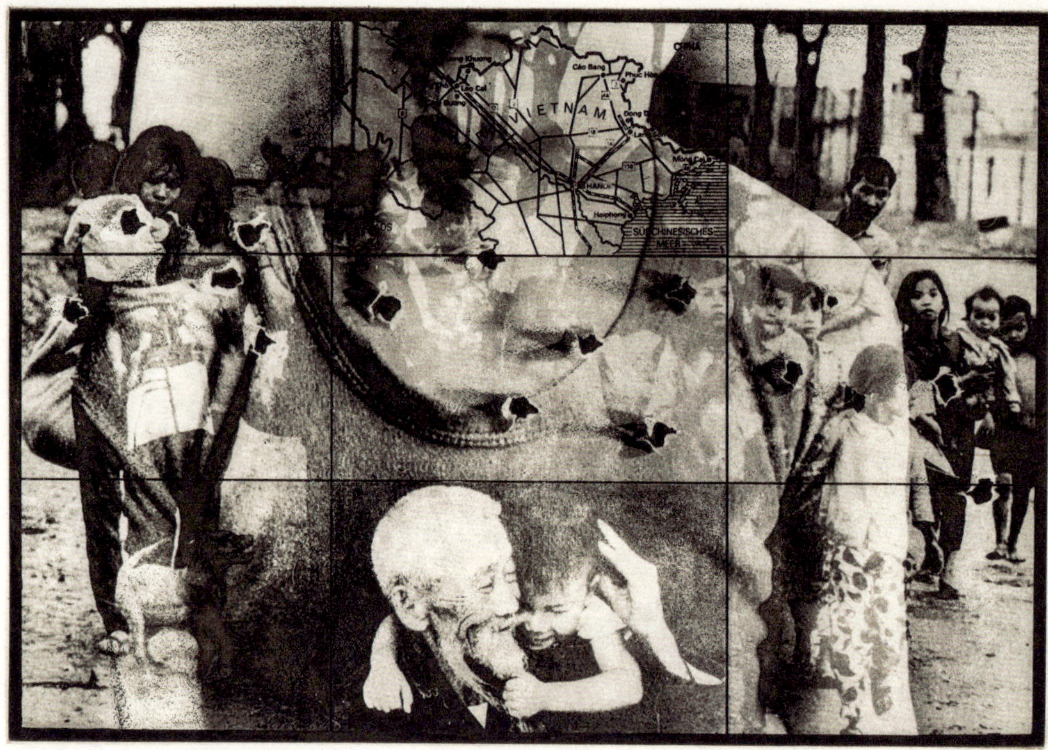

Joachim Jansong. February 17, 79, 1979, etching, photomontage, 39 × 53 cm, Kupferstich-Kabinett, Staatliche Kunstsammlungen Dresden, inv. no. A 1979–497

Fritz Cremer, Down With the Murderers of the Vietnamese People!, sheet 9 from the series *Vietnam*, 1967, lithograph, 50.4 × 73.5 cm, Kupferstich-Kabinett, Staatliche Kunstsammlungen Dresden, inv. no. A 1970–305

Ibrahim Hazimeh, Two Palestinian Children, 1971, brush in watercolors, 36 × 47.8 cm, Kupferstich-Kabinett, Staatliche Kunstsammlungen Dresden, inv. no. C 1973–73

That was, I don't want to say a liberation, but it was a new experience for me: aha, so colors can glow like this!

The artist Sigrid Noack on a trip to South Yemen organized by the Central Council of the Freie Deutsche Jugend (Free German Youth; East German youth organization) in 1983, interview as part of the research project *Art in Networks—The GDR and its Global Relations*, see p. 171.

Lea Grundig. Ships on a River Near Wuhan, 1960, brush, pen in ink, 50.2 × 69.8 cm, Kupferstich-Kabinett, Staatliche Kunstsammlungen Dresden, inv.no. C 1975–16

Nora Kaschuba, Jule Lagoda, Kerstin Schankweiler

"She wanted only something personal: to travel"— Mobility and Restriction of Artists in the GDR Era

Famously, the German Democratic Republic pursued the strict security of its national borders and limited the freedom of its citizens to travel. That also affected artists who lived and worked in the GDR. Many artists were nevertheless able to travel abroad. Permits could be granted for a wide range of reasons to travel, such as study trips, accompanying exhibitions, or in the context of cultural-policy projects. Documents such as travel applications, reports, and travel diaries in public and private archives provide evidence of such trips. Last but not least, works of art were produced during stays abroad or following them that assimilated personal experiences and impressions. Another important source for the present essay is interviews with artists conducted as part of the research project *Art in Networks: The GDR and its Global Relations*.[1]

The surviving travel applications make it clear that many artists wanted to discover the world. But files in archives also document the political and bureaucratic hurdles that stood in their way. It seems obvious that in the GDR trips abroad had a very special value against the backdrop of limited mobility. They moved within the tension between (lack of) freedom to travel, cultural policy, and private interests.

Research on the travel policy for artists in the GDR, which was determined above all by the Verband Bildender Künstler (VBK; Association of Visual Artists of the GDR) and the Ministry of Culture has been sparse thus far.[2] In a groundbreaking essay, Sigrid Hofer compiled the first case studies.[3] In the study she concentrated on trips to the West and observed that they were approved more often than common ideas about travel restrictions in the GDR would have led one to assume. With regard to trips outside Europe in particular, but also for trips to the Soviet Union or other countries of the Eastern Bloc, which were often organized as study trips or student exchanges, there is still great need for additional research.[4]

Traveling in the GDR System

The opportunities for artists to travel outside of the GDR was closely tied to the organization of the art system within the country. Artists with important positions in cultural policy had, as a rule, extensive travel privileges. For an artist such as Lea Grundig (1906–1977),

---

1   As part of the project *Art in Networks: The GDR and Its Global Relations, 1949–1990* at the Technische Universität Dresden under the direction of Kerstin Schankweiler in 2022, a digital research platform was created with contributions on the GDR's international relations in the fine arts. Numerous interviews with historical eyewitnesses were conducted: artinnetworks.web-space.tu-dresden.de. In addition to the authors of the present essay, the participants included Pauline Hohn, Elke Neumann, Anja Degner, Laura-Maria Schulze, and Janine Kläffling, whom we would like to thank sincerely here.

2   Sigrid Hofer: Die DDR im Westen. Von Reisekadern, renitenten Künstlern und diplomatischem Kalkül, in: Künstlerreisen: Fallbeispiele vom Mittelalter bis zur Gegenwart, eds. Andreas Tacke et al., Petersberg 2020, p. 233–245; Christian Saehrendt: Kunst im Kampf für das "Sozialistische Weltsystem". Auswärtige Kulturpolitik der DDR in Afrika und Nahost, Stuttgart, 2017; Barbara Tlusty, Silke Wagler: "Wir sahen interessante Gesichter hinter Melonenpyramiden". DDR-Künstler auf Reisen im Spiegel von Reisebildern aus dem Kunstfonds, in: Dresdener Kunstblätter 51 (2008), no. 4, p. 266–282. In addition, the theme was also addressed in the exhibition *Künstlerreisen in der DDR: Hinter dem Eisernen Vorhang* (Artists' Travels in the GDR—Behind the Iron Curtain) in 2019, curated by Cornelia Junge for the Kustodie der Universität Leipzig.

3   Hofer 2020 (note 2).

4   A research project, funded by the Fritz Thyssen Stiftung, has been working on this theme since April 2023: *Affektive Archive—Auslandsreisen von Künstler:innen zur Zeit der DDR* (Affective Archives—Journeys Abroad by Artists During the GDR Era) under the direction of Kerstin Schankweiler at the Technische Universität Dresden. On artists' trips to Latin America, see Marcus Kenzler: Der Blick in die andere Welt: Einflüsse Lateinamerikas auf die Bildende Kunst der DDR, Berlin 2012.

who was president of the VBK in the late 1960s, study trips to Cuba or the People's Republic of China were a matter of course.[5] Walter Womacka (1925–2010) made annual trips as the rector of the Kunsthochschule Weißensee and vice president of the VBK, including to Egypt, Indonesia, Columbia, and Ecuador. On them he was often negotiating on behalf of the VBK on agreements with foreign artists' associations and performing other functions of cultural diplomacy. A number of his works were produced in the context of his travels, from depictions of the population to a commissioned portrait of the Syrian dictator Hafiz al-Assad, which he painted after several days of sittings in Damascus in 1987.[6]

Artists without political positions, by contrast, often did not know until shortly before their departure whether a trip would be approved and found themselves confronted with the arbitrariness of the GDR bureaucracy. Despite the introduction of a travel system for cadres with centralized political control, decision-making processes were usually prolonged and not transparent.[7] The state often permitted or denied travel as a reward or sanction and sometimes even deliberately caused uncertainty to sow jealousy and mistrust.[8]

In addition to demanding political reliability from the applicants, financial criteria often played a role, because the GDR chronically lacked hard currency to fund stays in non-socialist economic areas. If a delegation had not initiated by the state, the artists generally had to cover travel costs themselves, or they had to be paid by the receiving institutions or hosts. Because currency exchange was at rates were unfavorable to and limited for citizens of the GDR, many artists simply lacked the money to travel. Even when the VBK was covering the costs, artists often had to accept many restrictions, such as reduction of the requested travel time or leaving family members behind was viewed as a kind of "bargaining chip" to ensure that travelers would not "flee the Republic." For example, the husband-and-wife painters Antje Fretwurst-Colberg (b. 1940) and Friedrich-Wilhelm Fretwurst (b. 1936) had to leave their children behind in East Berlin when traveling to Mexico in 1988. They had the opportunity to make the trip because another married couple from Mexico, the painter Carlos Kunte und and the sculptor Estela Ubando, had requested exchange partners for a visit to East Berlin. Two years earlier, Antje Fretwurst-Colberg and the artist Núria Quevedo (b. 1938) had been invited to represent the GDR at a cultural festival in Havana. There Antje Fretwurst-Colberg had learned Spanish and was therefore selected by the VBK for the exchange. She and her husband were able to visit cultural sites and museums in Mexico and study in depth the murals of the Communist artist Diego Rivera, who was famous in the GDR. On both trips, Antje Fretwurst-Colberg produced numerous watercolors and gouaches and wrote in retrospect: "This trip was a great experience and also very inspiring for our own artistic work."[9]

As in this example, artists were sometimes delegated by the VBK when travel opportunities arose as part of cultural exchange or a traveling exhibition. Invitations from institutions abroad could also provide an official occasion. Other artists actively sought trips abroad in order to expand their horizons through impressions outside the GDR. The painter Sigrid Noack (b. 1947), for example, read in the newspaper about a brigade from the Freie Deutsche Jugend (FDJ; Free German Youth) in Cuba. She asked the central committee of the FDJ and her trip was approved in 1983—albeit to South Yemen rather than Cuba, without giving the reasons. There she was urged above all to document in paintings the work that the FDJ was doing there. In 1987, she completed the large-format triptych *Brigade der Freundschaft in der VDR Jemen* (Brigade of Friendship in the People's Democratic Republic of Yemen),

---

5   On Lea Grundig's trip to China, see p. 84 in this volume.
6   See Walter Womacka: Farbe bekennen. Erinnerungen, Berlin 2004.
7   The GDR's travel cadre consisted of people selected by the state who were regarded as politically reliable and therefore had special travel privileges. See Jens Niederhut: Die Reisekader. Auswahl und Disziplinierung einer privilegierten Minderheit in der DDR, Leipzig 2005.
8   Hofer 2020 (note 2), p. 236.
9   E-mail correspondence with Antje Fretwurst-Colberg, June 2022: https://artinnetworks.webspace.tu-dresden.de/de/beitraege/reisen-der-kuenstlerin-antje-fretwurst-colberg (accessed on: 6.7.2023).

showing East German and Yemenite men together at work and leisure. In addition to this commissioned work, the sketches she had made in South Yemen were used for other paintings after she returned. In an interview she stated: "That was for me … I don't want to say liberation, but it was a new experience for me: Aha, colors can glow like this as well!" and confirmed that her impressions from the trip had a lasting influence on her painting.[10] By contrast, concerning the rules for behavior when traveling that were imposed on artists by the state, which sometimes genuinely limited personal contact abroach, she said: "I would have liked very much to meet colleagues there; I knew there were one or two near Aden, and I believe that one of them was even a sculptor, but every time that I brought it up, it was not important."[11] The VBK precisely stipulated the powers artists had when traveling. Before leaving, they had to sign a so-called directive that set out rules and tasks for the stay. Artists were required to report to the relevant GDR embassies and did not have the right to establish contact with foreign artists' associations on their own. After their return, they had to submit to the VBK a detailed report on their activities on their trip. These travel reports illustrate not only the bureaucratic surveillance and nannying but also the state's interest in information gained on the trips. Artists were thus always subjected to the political framework and were influenced in complicated ways by both the domestic politics and the foreign cultural policy of the GDR.[12]

Traveling on Behalf of Friendship between Peoples

One foreign-policy goal of initiating and permitting travel was to increase "relationships of friendship between peoples" to other countries as part of bilateral cultural agreements or actions of solidarity.[13] The graphic artists Peter Westphal (b. 1938) and Wolfgang Speer (1926–2015), for example, made a study trip to the "brother country" of North Vietnam in 1970 with the support of the Ministry of Culture in order to make portraits to record their impressions of the population at war against the USA and South Vietnam. Their five-year project with other artists at the graphic-art workshop in Pankow brought in more than a million marks in donations for Vietnam. Inspired by the Afro-Asian Solidarity Committee of the GDR, a portfolio of prints of selected works was produced after the trip and sold on various occasions.[14] Solidarity with socialist-oriented North Vietnam was to

10   Interview with Sigrid Noack, June 29, 2022: https://artinnetworks.webspace.tu-dresden.de/de/beitraege/kuenstlerinnen-reise-in-den-suedjemen (accessed on: 6.7.2023).
11   Ibid.
12   A detailed first account of the structural and political conditions under which artists from the GDR could travel to Western Europe in particular can be found in Hofer 2020 (note 2).
13   On this, see the essay by Christian Saehrendt in this volume, p. 37–42.
14   Interview with Peter Westphal, May 20, 2022: https://artinnetworks.webspace.tu-dresden.de/de/beitraege/sechswoechige-reise-der-grafiker-peter-westphal-und-wolfgang-speer-durch-vietnam (accessed on: 6.7.2023); the graphic portfolio *Vietnam—Das geht dich an!* (1970) contains twenty reproductions based on lithographs by Wolfgang Speer and Peter Westphal and was offered at a "solidarity price" of fifteen (GDR) marks.

be communicated artistically as well.

In other cases, trips were possible against the backdrop of "socialist internationalism" and "anti-imperialist solidarity" with (formerly) colonized countries. The artist Wolfgang Eckardt traveled to Maputo on the occasion of the group exhibition *Three Artists from Rostock* in 1986. He gave the Ministry of Culture a portrait bust he had made of Samora Machel, the recently deceased cofounder of the FRELIMO independence movement and the first president of Mozambique, along with a donation to Mozambican artists in solidarity from the VBK.[15]

Artist exchange in the name of "friendship between peoples" did not by any means move unilaterally from the GDR abroad. The GDR itself was also a travel destination for artists. Large-scale events such as international plenaries and art festivals regularly offered occasions for artists to visit the GDR. The *INTERGRAFIK* triennial was particular important in this, inviting international participants to East Berlin from 1965 to 1990 under the guiding idea of "artistic commitment to peace, humanism, understanding between peoples, and social progress."[16] Trips to other artist centers in the GDR were sometimes organized for the guests of the triennial during their stay.

Contacts to movements and organizations for political liberation were also bolstered as part of *INTERGRAFIK*. During their visit to the GDR in 1973, for example, the artist Tamam Al Akhal (b. 1935) and her husband, Ismail Shammout (1930–2006), the director of the arts and culture section of the Palestinian Liberation Organization (PLO) in Lebanon, spoke of inviting artists from the GDR to Beirut.[17] Six years later, a five-member delegation traveled to Lebanon. Edmund Bechtle (b. 1947), Falko Behrendt (b. 1951), Christian Heinze (b. 1941), Uwe Bullmann (1945–2016), and Günther Rechn (b. 1944) were supposed to address the concerns of the PLO and of Palestinians who had been exiled or had fled during the war of 1948. They recorded their impressions in sketches and photographs that they later turned into paintings and prints. Uwe Bullmann remarked in retrospect: "A flood of completely new stimuli experienced in Lebanon's situation in 1979 and in 1981 must be processed and integrated into my own artistic program."[18] On a second trip the five artists made to Beirut in 1981, works were presented in the PLO's Al Karamah exhibition venue and a year later toured the GDR. Travel in the context of cultural policy could also lead to personal connections as is clear from several case studies. In Lebanon, Günther Rechn met probably the most famous Palestinian graphic artist, Mustafa al-Hallaj (1938–2002), and was enthusiastic about his works.[19] His own painting *Hommage à Mustafa Hallaj* expresses his personal appreciation and depicts the artist, who was then living in exile in Beirut, as a man without a homeland sitting in a barren landscape surrounded by mysterious figures.

Travel Bans and State Capriciousness

The dark side of the artist travels outlined here is the important theme of prevented and banned trips. Faced with repression, many artists presumably only imagined traveling and never applied for it in the first place because it would have been hopeless. The travel restrictions in the GDR affected artists in many ways. In addition to private interests, travel abroad was an important way to exchange with the international contemporary art scene, to see works in the original, and to increase their own fame. Many artists thus sought opportunities to establish international contacts in other ways or actively challenged travel bans.

15   Rostocker Künstler in Maputo. Wolfgang Eckardt zeigte Büste von Samora Machel, in: Neues Deutschland, November 12, 1987, p. 4.
16   Symposium zur Intergrafik '84, in: Berliner Zeitung, June 7, 1984, p. 2. On *INTERGRAFIK*, see the essay by Annabel Ruckdeschel in this volume, p. 133–139.
17   Interview with Annabel Ruckdeschel, October 14, 2022: https://artinnetworks.webspace.tu-dresden.de/de/beitraege/annabel-ruckdeschel (accessed on: 6.7.2023).
18   Uwe Bullmann in: Engagement Palästina, exh. cat. Galerie Kunstsammlung Cottbus, Cottbus 1981, p. 31.
19   Günther Rechn in conversation with the participants in the Art in Networks project, April 1, 2022 (note 1).

Günther Rechn, Homage to Mustafa Hallaj, 1981, oil on canvas, 68 × 98 cm, Museum Utopie und Alltag, Beeskow

For some, mail art became a substitute for travel. Artists throughout the world exchanged works of art in letter format by mail to cultivate friendships. Because the mailings were often political and subversive, the Stasi often persecuted mail artists and intercepted many letters. Nevertheless, global networks formed, so that artists from the GDR corresponded, among others, with artists in other Eastern Bloc countries, Western Europe, and North and South America.[20] According to the artist and collector Lutz Wohlrab (b. 1959), mail art was intended "to overcome [...] international [...] borders, the borders of language, of cultures, national borders, political borders ... freedom was the most important thing to us."[21] In some cases, postal contacts even led to personal ones. For example, the Canadian mail art and performance artist Anna Banana (b. 1940) visited East Berlin in 1978 and met friends such as the artist Karla Sachse (b. 1950). This resulted in forms of artistic collaboration that outlived the decline of the GDR.[22]

Contentious discussions of travel restrictions were not limited to the subculture of mail art but were also the subject of heated debates within state cultural institutions. Public and private criticism of artists who were unjustly granted travel privileges is exemplified by the case of the artist Annemirl Bauer (1939–1989).[23] Although she did not reject the GDR fundamentally, in her work Bauer became increasingly critical of SED policies, represented feminist positions, and addressed border and travel policies, among other things. Since the 1960s, she had been able to undertake study trips to France and Eastern bloc countries, which she assimilated in numerous collages and drawings. For example, she combined impressions of French towns and everyday scenes she had observed with typical travel documents such as stamps, clippings from postcards and travel guides, and found materials. She drew a self-portrait in felt-tip pen on a map of Paris and added a collage of newspaper clippings. The bright colors and delicate linework of her travel drawings contrast with other work and convey a feeling of lightness as opposed to the "imprisonment" in the GDR.[24] In 1983, her application for another trip to Tarascon in France was denied. In a letter to the president of the VBK, Willi Sitte, in 1984, Bauer then demanded that the GDR grant universal freedom to travel: "The independence of my thinking and acting is increasingly more or less nonexistent as a result of lifelong violent limitation by means of noninformation and isolation. For that reason, I urgently demand, first, that my daughter and I be granted free and unlimited entry and exit travel and, second, a program for the next three years specified in writing that this obvious right of unhindered travel be possible for all strata of the population."[25]

Bauer's commitment was sanctioned by temporary expulsion from the association, which went hand in hand with extensive repression and surveillance by the Stasi. The artist expressed her situation in another self-portrait that sharply contrasts with the one from Paris.

20   On mail art, see the essay by Elena Shtromberg in this volume, p. 49–55.

21   Interview with Lutz Wohlrab, October 7, 2022: https://artinnetworks.webspace.tu-dresden.de/de/beitraege/kunst-per-post-der-mail-artist-und-sammler-lutz-wohlrab (accessed on: 6.7.2023).

22   See the exhibition by Anna Banana, *Proof Positive Germany Is Going Bananas*, Salon am Moritzplatz, Berlin, which was held in November 2020 as a new version of an exhibition in 1993.

23   Inken Dohrmann: Der Fall Annemirl Bauer, in: Eingegrenzt—Ausgegrenzt. Bildende Kunst und Parteiherrschaft in der DDR 1961–1989, ed. Hannelore Offner and Klaus Schröder, Berlin 2000, p. 311–367.

24   Anke Paula Böttcher: Zeichen wie atmen. Gedanken zu Annemirl Bauer, in: Annemirl Bauer: Ich möchte kein gefangener Vogel im Käfig sein, ed. Ulrike Kremeier and Annette Tietz, Cottbus and Berlin 2015, p. 74–80, here p. 75.

25   Excerpt from the application submitted to Willi Sitte, March 4, 1984, quoted in: In meinem eigenen Lande. Die Malerin und Dissidentin Annemirl Bauer, ed. Kristina Volke on behalf of the Deutscher Bundestag, Berlin 2012, p. 68–72.

Annemirl Bauer, Untitled (Self Portrait on Paris City Map), 1980s, collage and photography, 50 × 50 cm, Nachlassarchiv Annemirl Bauer

In it she is seen behind bars surrounded by words reminiscent of an accusation in court: "Argument: Application without personal concern is unconstitutional. She wanted only something personal: to travel. Therefore excluded egoist! The butchered virgin."

Summary

These few examples already make it clear that no generalizing statements can be made about the conditions for travel by artists. Moreover, both the opportunities for travel and its personal importance for individual artists' careers differed. Trips ranged in a spectrum from state assignments to study trips and vacations, but they were rarely unencumbered and free. Many artists were denied them entirely. The theme of mobility in the art scene of the GDR must be considered very broadly to paint a complete picture. That absolutely includes imagined and prevented trips as well as resistance to restrictions on travel freedom in the GDR, works of art sent traveling or made in the context of travels. We are therefore dealing with very heterogenous policies, practices, and aesthetics of artists' travels in the GDR era.

Although the state strictly distinguished between "socialist" and "nonsocialist" countries, that was not necessarily reflected in the destinations of approved trips, which were subject to a complex interplay of political interests. In future research, the ambiguity between the state framework and personal organization of trips, contacts made and random encounters abroad, must be outlined in greater detail on a broader basis of materials and through archival research and interviews with historical eyewitnesses. Last but not least, the production of art in connection with travels has received little attention thus far even though a wealth of works in public and private collections testify to the relevance of the theme for artists in the GDR era.

Annemirl Bauer, The Naked Emperor Sends his Regards!, 1984,
gouache on paper, 74.3 × 51.2 cm, Nachlassarchiv Annemirl Bauer

Bernhard Kretzschmar, Untitled (Chinese Landscape), 1954, pencil, 45.2 × 68 cm,
Kupferstich-Kabinett, Staatliche Kunstsammlungen Dresden, inv. no. C 1983-649

Lea Grundig. [the girl] Phom-Renk, 1963, pen in ink, watercolors, 58.2 × 32.8 cm, Kupferstich-Kabinett, Staatliche Kunstsammlungen Dresden, inv. no. C 1975-12

26
FiDEL
INSTITUTO CUBANO DEL ARTE E INDUSTRIA CINEMATOGRAFICOS

156

Before my journey back home, the Berlin Wall
was built while I was in Cuba. Then came
the return trip, and the stopover was in Canada.
The door was open with the sign 'for emigration'.
And they were watching us to see if we were
scooting. And there I was, standing in front of it,
thinking, 'Now I'm leaving.' But I couldn't. It was
a very simple thing, a moral thing. When you saw
what they had planned and were enthusiastic
about it [...] so I went home, to the GDR, to
the Wall.

The photographer Thomas Billhardt on his return journey from Cuba to the GDR in 1961,
interview as part of the research project *Art in Networks—The GDR and its Global Relations*,
see p. 171.

The Missed Seminar, an intervention of the research department of the Dresden State Art Collections in conjunction with the project *Decolonizing Socialism: Entangled Internationalism* at the Albertinum, Dresden, 30.3.–4.11.2023, photo: Alexander Peitz

Doreen
Mende

Entangled Internationalisms—Entangled Generations: Perspectives from Research at the Staatliche Kunstsammlungen Dresden across all Collections

"The next generation will grow out of it", is something I hear in conversations about the undead GDR at times. But why should the people in the eastern part of Germany be so different from those in Chile, Cuba, Ethiopia, Ghana, Indonesia, Iran, Namibia, Palestine, Post-Yugoslavia, South Africa, or Vietnam, who have all been influenced by post-revolutionary upheavals or system change since the 1960s, albeit in different contexts? Knowledge, trauma, and memory are passed on from generation to generation, generating symptoms that keep on transforming until the ambivalent and the suppressed are acknowledged.

In the post-GDR context, aspects such as the experience of social overload and political dejection after the euphoria of 1990, rejected applications for grants, and the handling of institutional silence must be validated. For this, unarchived conversations are just as relevant as studies, academic essays, books, and exhibitions. If lived experience is recognized as a category of knowledge alongside museological and academic inquiry, so-called 'situated research' can avoid such categories as "the first project" or "the first exhibition". Rather, it is aware of the transgenerationality of this subject. It asks, for instance, why it has been so difficult in the first two decades following the year 1990 to not only gain institutional recognition but also to find the critical self-awareness for a GDR art history or for artistic networks of international solidarity—including at the Staatliche Kunstsammlungen Dresden (SKD; Dresden State Art Collections). Since 2008, the rights and wrongs of the GDR are being documented systematically in the SKD's project "DAPHNE" which surveys so-called "Schlossbergungen" (castle salvages)—expropriations of movable properties during the agrarian reform in the Soviet occupation zone from the fall of 1945 onwards. The focus of this endeavor is on property rights issues rather than artistic processes of the collections' histories, and yet this provenance research is considered as exemplary by the SKD. What does this mean for a reevaluation of art history? Why was the incessant argument over the assessment of the complex spectrum of state-approved and dissident art in the GDR—the so-called "Bilderstreit" (controversy over the significance and evaluation of art from the GDR)—reignited in Dresden in 2017? Why was it that, when I started working at the SKD in 2021, the directors of the collections were highly esteemed colleagues and international experts, but lacked any personal experience of revolution or upheaval? Why did the updating of work titles in the SKD's online collection trigger a media backlash in Saxony, motivated by identitarian politics? Might the debate in Dresden stir up memories of the renaming of streets, squares, and schools in Eastern Germany after 1990? The real-life consequences of these memories are more complex than a course of study, an occupation, or a lifetime.

This transgenerationality that is interrupted and suppressed and at the same time evident in archives also applies to the research project *Decolonizing Socialism: Entangled Internationalism* which is an undertaking of the Master's program *Critical Curatorial Cybermedia Research Practices* (CCC RP)—a cooperation of the Haute école d'art et de design HEAD Genève and the chair of Urban Studies at Basel University. *Decolonizing Socialism* is funded by the Swiss National Science Foundation. Under my supervision, it has initiated various case studies of entangled art internationalisms in the GDR in order to enable contemporary interrogation. Since 2021 there has been increased cooperation with the SKD's Department of Research, and the project's focus has shifted to curatorial and artistic methods of transhistorical inquiry. Close links have been established with partners in Ethiopia, India, Ghana, Mozambique, and Namibia in preparation of a three-part exhibition called *Sequences: Entangled Internationalisms* at the Albertinum which will start in 2024.

Similar to the exhibition *Revolutionary Romances? Global Art Histories in the GDR*, the series *Sequences: Entangled Internationalisms* works with historical case studies which situate the GDR in the context of the global Cold War but can neither be found in the archives and collections of the SKD nor in the history of the GDR in and of itself. In their respective contexts, these case studies operate as specific framings that allow a contemporary look at the collections in Dresden from geographies in Asia or Africa that were connected with the GDR, through the use of oral history, counter-archives, and transhistorical knowledge. With its systematic record of a transcultural GDR art history through the works of artists such as Martha Ketsela or Mankew Valente Mahumana that are found in the collections, *Revolutionary Romances?* makes an enormously important and overdue contribution to the visualization of a collection history that features a multitude of diasporic forms of knowledge and geo-cultural entanglements which were rewritten by the museum—in its historical function as an institution that contributed to the generation of culture and national identity—as a *white* history. But *Sequences: Entangled Internationalisms*, does not presume any specific collection nor institutional history. It uses three case studies to examines various geopolitical entanglements of the GDR around the world with the goal of decentering the GDR: Here, historical moments in the present of India or Ghana in their entanglements with the GDR serve as starting points that thanks to their forms of practice and their networks of artists, filmmakers, and researchers reveal an underlying entangled structure. The artist Vinit Agarwal, who has been a research fellow of the research project for years, found an appropriate label for this kind of entangled internationalism when he talked about "traversing the GDR". As an example in case, between March and November 2023, the SKD Department of Research staged a display case intervention titled *The Missed Seminar* at the Albertinum, alongside the hanging of works from the European Avantgarde: It begins with the friendship of the well-known actor and singer Paul Robeson and the feminist, photographer, and anthropologist Eslanda Robeson (both protagonists of the so-called Harlem Renaissance as well as public sympathisers of the communist movements during the Cold War) to the Marxist German-Jewish philosopher Franz Loeser and Diana Loeser, presenter of the GDR television program *English for you*. Based on their encounters in Leipzig, East Berlin, and Prague around 1963, *The Missed Seminar* poses the question: What can the friendship between the Robesons and the Loesers teach us today in terms of the linkage of struggles against fascism, colonialism, and antisemitism?

All three parts of the exhibition series *Sequences: Entangled Internationalisms* follow a multidimensional research method: Firstly, it presents a historical moment or case study in the form of a piece of art, a film, or a piece of architecture. Secondly, it reconstructs the historical context of the case study with the help of documents from the archives. Thirdly, these archive records are transformed into the materials needed to create an "archival metabolism", as we call the method of transhistorical research as part of the project's exhibition practice, which addresses the question of the transgenerationality of the historical documents' very own materiality. Fourthly, contemporary artists devise works in response to the case studies. And fifthly, selected objects from the collections of the SKD that can be understood as resonating with the case studies are shown each time.

The exhibition *Till the Sun Rises* contains *Sequence 1*, curated by Vinit Agarwal, founder of the Oralities Research Lab in Jaipur, India, in dialogue with the artists Aarti Sunder and Moses März. *Till the Sun Rises* mobilises the film *OYOYO* (1980) by Indian filmmaker Chetna Vora, who studied in the GDR. Sunder and März activate *OYOYO* as an archive of

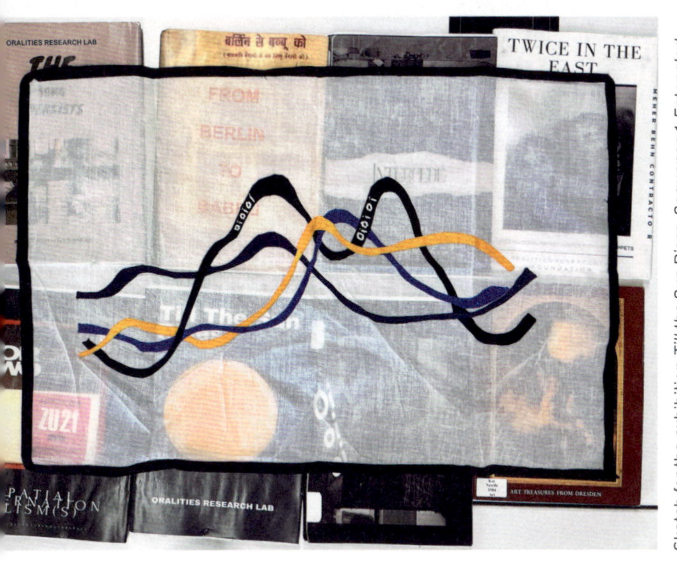

Sketch for the exhibition *Till the Sun Rises. Sequence 1: Entangled Internationalism*, created by Hatheli Sansthan Women's Cooperative at SWRC Dhanau, Barmer, Rajasthan in India based on the research of Vinit Agarwal in conversation with Moses März and Aarti Sunder, based on the film *OYOYO* (1980) by Chetna Vora, Oralities Research Lab, Jaipur, September 2023

internationalisms by tracing the students portrayed in the film, from Ethiopia, Chile, Guinea-Bissau, Mongolia, and other countries, during their time in the GDR. How can a film help us understand an entangled internationalism today? What words, sounds, and images were generated through it? Corresponding objects from the SKD's Archiv der Avantgarden (Archive of the Avant-Gardes) and from the Puppentheatersammlung (Puppet Theatre Collection) are also displayed.

Sequence 2 carries the title *The Year 1983* and is based on the curatorial concept of sociologist and critic Zoé Samudzi. This sequence is realised in dialogue with the artist Tuli Mekondjo, who was born to Namibian parents in exile in Angola, and examines the GDR's solidarity with the South West African People's Organisation (SWAPO), a Marxist liberation movement that fought for Namibia's independence. The sequence focuses on the way the genocide of the Herero and Nama peoples, perpetrated by German forces between 1904 and 1908 in what is Namibia today, was commemorated in the GDR during the 1980s. Together with the transdisciplinary group Forensis, it also envisions a reverse restitution of materials of German provenance which have remained in Namibia to this day. In cooperation with the artist and designer Nontsikelelo Mutiti, a visual-spatial reflection on the transgenerationality of archive materials emerges, while objects from the Staatliche Ethnographische Sammlungen Sachsen (Saxonian State Collections of Ethnography) are also foreseen for this sequence.

The exhibition *A World After its Own Image* will show *Sequence 3*, curated by Kwasi Ohene-Ayeh, member of the BlaxTARLINES collective, in dialogue with the artist Adjoa Armah, founder of the Saman archive—both of whom are from Ghana—, as well as with filmmaker and author Jihan El-Thari. First of all, it traces the construction project of the government printing office in the city of Tema in southern Ghana under the country's first president, Kwame Nkrumah. The building's architecture was designed in the GDR by a collective around civil engineer Kurt Fiedler at the VEB Industrieprojektierung Leipzig (state-owned company for industrial project planning) and the building itself inaugurated at Nkrumah's 55th birthday in 1964. Secondly, the sequence examines the transgenerational traces of the film *The Black Star* shot director Joachim Hellwig. Hellwig of the state-owned DEFA Documentary Film studios in various locations in Ghana in 1964. On top of all that, objects from the SKD's Archive of the Avant-Gardes as well as the Green Vault are earmarked for this stage of the exhibition series.

Sequences: Entangled Internationalisms is not about another suppression of the GDR, but an uncovering of its transgenerational dialogues within a global network. The upheaval around the year 1990 does not only affect the people in the eastern part of Germany, but is being processed by geographies and generations around the world to this day. If this turning point—which marks the creation of a "before" and an "after"—is treated in a transformative way, it leads to new methodological approaches that bring the realities of post-communism and those of the postcolonial worlds closer together than geographies that are trained to perpetuate the traditions of a modern capitalist world. In researching the geopolitical contexts of this turning point, the Dresden State Art Collections are transformed into resonating bodies that offer the possibility of understanding materialistic-historical entanglements from our present-day perspective and of shaping them for the future.

One thing holds true for both *Revolutionary Romances?* and *Sequences: Entangled Internationalisms*: Overcoming the transformational experience of 1990 could no longer be understood as the struggle for recognition, sovereignty of interpretation, and continuities of the modern age, but has the potential to mobilize a variety of methods for an entangled production of knowledge. The decolonization of socialism along with its internationalisms and its acceptance as a historical reality (e. g. in the GDR) corresponds to a practice of decentralization, denationalization, and de-isolation that exceeds the scale of a single generation: It practices a form of "In-der-Welt-Sein" (Being-in-the-world) while being fully aware of its upheavals.

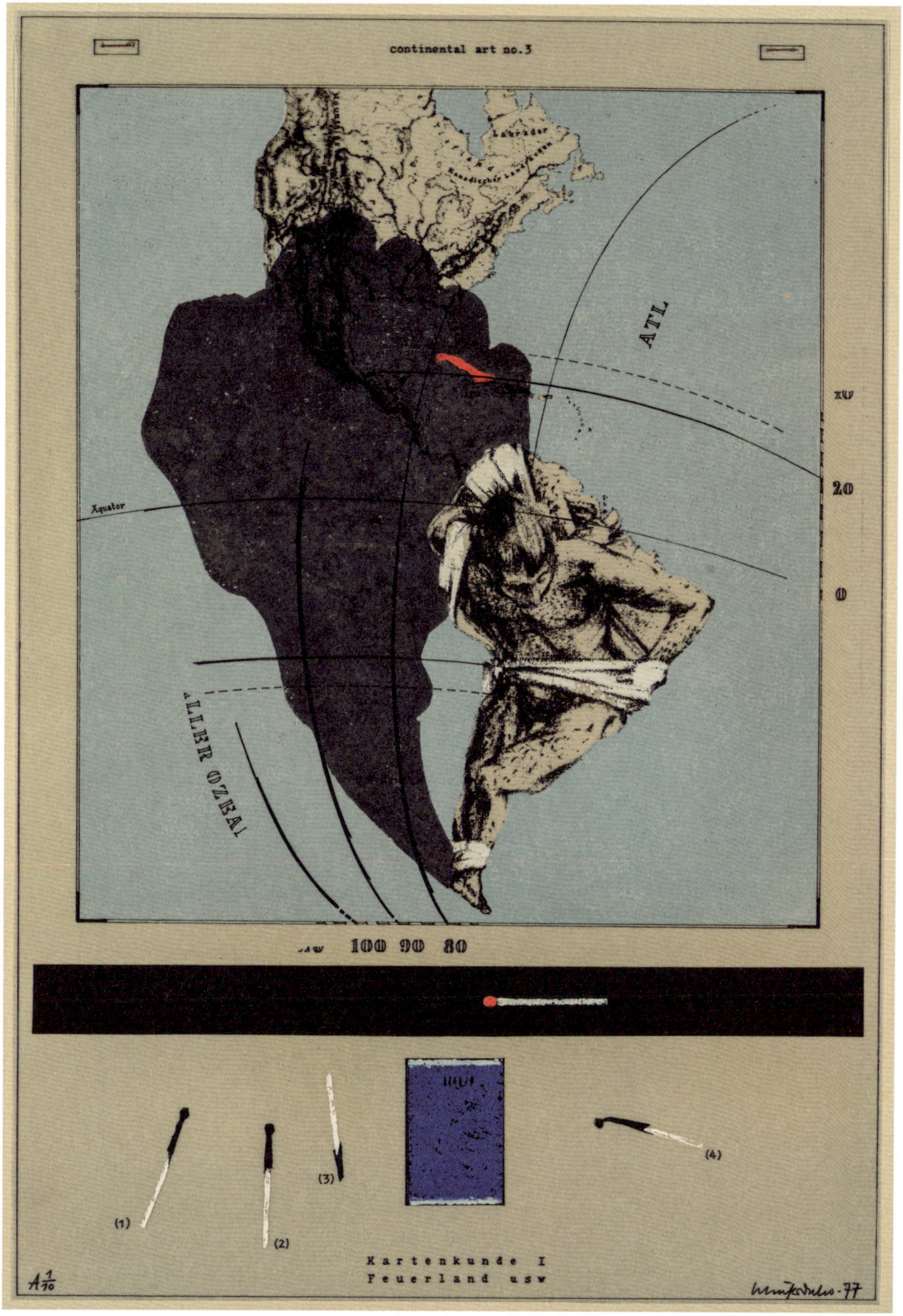

Jürgen Schieferdecker, Continental art no. 3, Cartography I, Tierra del Fuego etc., 1977, color letterpress on plan film, mounted on olive-bleached paper, 46 × 32 cm, Kupferstich-Kabinett, Staatliche Kunstsammlungen Dresden, inv. no. A 1984–24

Guillermo Deisler, Diagonal Stream of Letters, from the series *Visual Poetry*, n. d., screen print in two colors on yellowish paper, 14.9 × 10 cm, Kupferstich-Kabinett, Staatliche Kunstsammlungen Dresden, inv. no. B 1988–607

Chile 2/4 erstes Stadium
Ralf Winkler 79
LEO

It would be great if art from the GDR were studied more—not just from a political or ideological point of view, but also from an art historical perspective and in the context of European and pan-German art.

The artist Michael Touma on the reception of art from the GDR, interview as part of the research project *Art in Networks—The GDR and its Global Relations*, see p. 171.

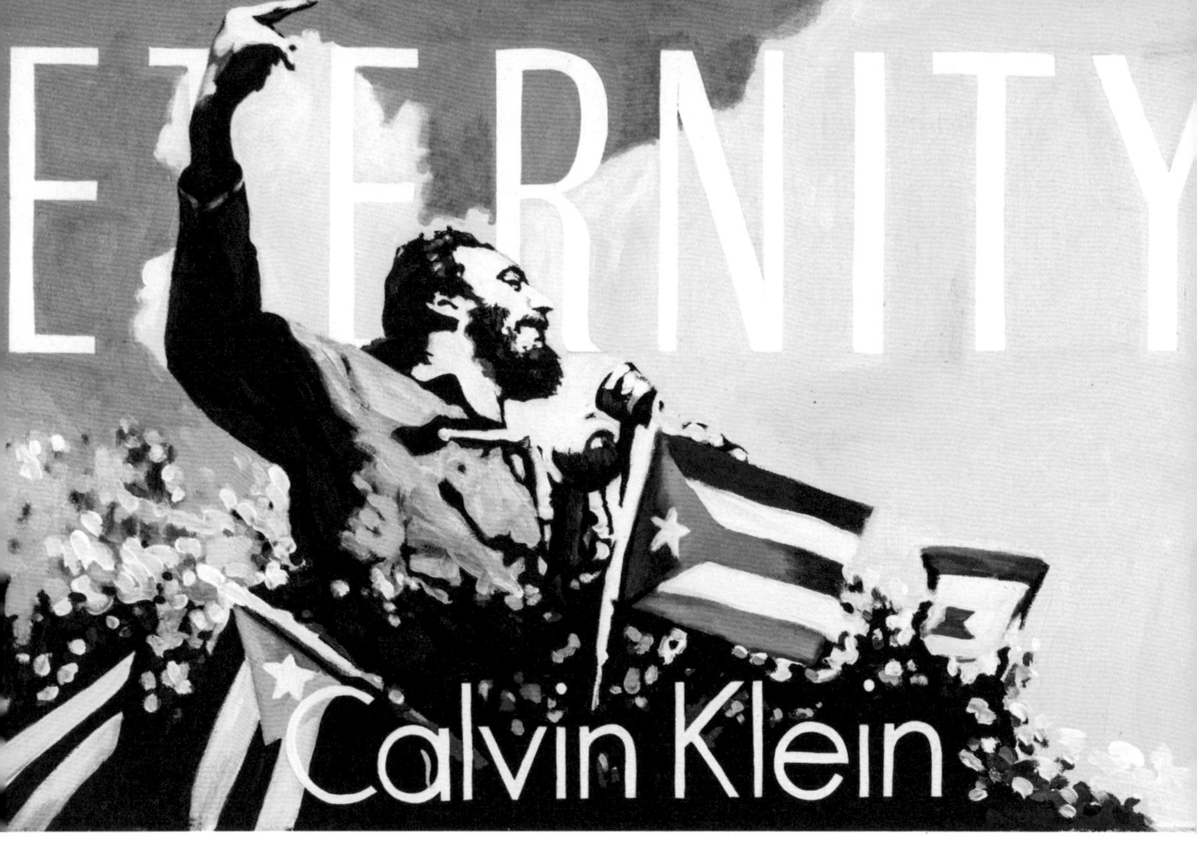

José Toirac, Eternity, 1996, oil on canvas, 60 × 90.5 cm, Ludwig Forum Aachen, Ludwig Collection, Loan Peter and Irene Ludwig Foundation

Jürgen Nagel, Parchim, school, 1986, silver gelatine paper, 28.5 × 39.2 cm,
Kupferstich-Kabinett, Staatliche Kunstsammlungen Dresden, inv. no. D 1990–129
The slogan on the four posters runs: "We are learning for the peace [in the world]."

Art in Networks—The GDR and its Global Relations
Digital research platform of the TU Dresden on the international contacts of the GDR in art

The project makes visible the connections between artists, museums and other cultural actors between the GDR and countries in Africa, Asia and Latin America and investigates the global networks that developed in the process. Individual case studies are used to examine how forms of private and institutional artistic exchange were shaped.

Videos by and with the following people already have been published:

Abed Abdi
Peter Albert
Nadine Atallah
Katrin Bahr
Valentin Bauer
Thomas Billhardt
Giselher Blesse
Wolfgang Bruhm
Clementine Butler-Gallie
Teresa Casanueva
Jennifer Chert
Erich Enge
Mikael Eriksson
Lena Geuer
Emmanuel Guiragossian
Peter Hartmann
Sabine Herrmann
Veit Hofmann
Klaus Killisch
Harald Kirschner
Hans-Ulrich Mönnig
Yvette Mutumba
Lea Marie Nienhoff
Sigrid Noack
César Olhagaray

Gaelle Prodhon
Ellen Pupeter
Mona Ragy Enayat
Juliane Richter
Annabel Ruckdeschel
Karla Sachse
Christian Saehrendt
Hans Scheuerecker
Hans-Jorg Schirmbeck
Sonya Schönberger
Elena Shtromberg
Siska
Gerlint Söder
Oliver Sukrow
Sophie Thorak
Michael Touma
Arlette Quỳnh-Anh Trần
Võ Hồng Chương-Đài
Dieter Weise
Angelika Weißbach
Peter Westphal
Lutz Wohlrab
Winfried Wolk

The platform is accessable at:
https://artinnetworks.webspace.tu-dresden.de/en

and Robert Rehfeldt: Leonhard Frank Duch, Clemente Padín

The assertion of claims pursuant to section 60 UrhG for the reproduction of images of works is carried out by VG Bild-Kunst. It was not possible to identify the rights holders of the images in all cases.

Imprint
This publication accompanies the exhibition
Revolutionary Romances?
Global Art Histories in the GDR
Albertinum, Staatliche Kunstsammlungen Dresden, 4 November 2023–2 June 2024

Cooperation partners
Kunstfonds, Kupferstich-Kabinett /
Staatliche Kunstsammlungen Dresden

Lenders
GRASSI Museum für Völkerkunde zu Leipzig
Hochschule für Bildende Künste Dresden
Kunstfonds, Staatliche Kunstsammlungen Dresden
Kunstgewerbemuseum, Staatliche Kunstsammlungen Dresden
Kunststiftung DZ Bank, Frankfurt a. M.
Kupferstich-Kabinett, Staatliche Kunstsammlungen Dresden
Ludwig Forum für Internationale Kunst Aachen
Museum für Sächsische Volkskunst und Puppentheatersammlung, Staatliche Kunstsammlungen Dresden

Exhibition
Staatliche Kunstsammlungen Dresden
Director general: Marion Ackermann
Managing director: Dirk Burghardt
Director Albertinum: Hilke Wagner
Project idea: Kathleen Reinhardt (curator at the Albertinum until November 2022)
Curator of the exhibition: Mathias Wagner
Curatorial assistence: Pauline Hohn, Martin Buhlig
Translation: Katherine Vanovitch, Kennedy-Unglaub Translations, Martin Buhlig
Education and mediation: Sophie Hundbiss, Laurentius Alvin in cooperation with Linda Dietrich; head of department: Claudia Schmidt

Christin Finger (Kultur Aktiv e.V.), Verena Böll; Marí Emily Bohley und Julia Eberth, Hung Cao The und Vuong Tuan Hai, Bela Alvarez, and Montserrat Butter, Moussa Mbarek, Janina Kracht, and other contemporary witnesses and artists
Outreach and society: Sandra Janßen; head of department: Tanja Schomaker, Christine Gerbich
Kupferstich-Kabinett: Björn Egging; director: Stephanie Buck
Kunstfonds: Barbara Tlusty, Anné Seipel, Sylvia Lemke, Alejandro Caturla Peirats, Janine Wagler; head of department: Silke Wagler
Research department: Doreen Mende
Hochschule für Bildende Künste Dresden: Sven Barnick; rector: Oliver Kossack
Exhibition management: Catrin Dietrich; head of department: Christin Wähner, Jiři Fajt
Restoration supervision / paintings: Maria Körber, Michael Schweiger; head of department: Elisabeth Schlesinger, Christoph Schölzel
Restoration supervision / sculpture: Lydia Emmeline Decker, Irene Pamer-Gatzsche, Luise Albrecht; head of department: Stephanie Exner
Restoration supervision / Kupferstich-Kabinett: Olaf Simon, Thomas Woite, Ines Beyer; head of department: Wiebke Schneider
Restoration supervision / Kunstfonds: Judith Steinke, Barbara Schinko; head of department: Silke Wagler
Restoration supervision / Hochschule für Bildende Künste Dresden: Ivo Mohrmann, assisted by students of art technology, conservation and restoration of art and cultural heritage
Office of the director of the Albertinum: Flavia Sommer
Collection management / paintings: Alexandra Schellenberg, assisted by Niklas Röthig
Collection management / sculpture: Jürgen Lange
Accounting and controlling: Olena Kühn, Manuela Voß; head of department: Elke Ullmann
Law and organization: Christopher Culmann, Laura Krömer, Dietmar Gebauer, Kai Hoffmann; head of department: Michael Geißdorf

Fundraising: Nina C. Illgen
Media and communication: Nina Schwarzenberger, Thabea Knoops; head of department:
Holger Liebs
Social media: Anika Lautenschläger,
Christina Hoffmann, Andreas Diesend
voices online platform: Lisa-Marie Gutte,
Leonhard Wolf; head of department:
Jacob Franke
Marketing: Petra Baum, Anne Böttger; head
of department: Doreen Scherfke
Personnel management: Manja Noack,
Denise Drutschmann; head of department:
Andrea Hanschmann
Event managment: Anne Böttger,
Wenke Ladewig
Facility management/IT: Nico Bachmann,
Ralph Kunze, Cai Schneider, Jens Wolf,
Martin Zavesky; head of department:
Michael John
Security: Holm Eberlein, Gero Graubner;
head of department: Ralph Krüger
Facility management Albertinum:
Tamás Burunkai
Exhibition architecture: KKS-Architektur +
Gestaltung, Dresden/Hagen Engicht,
Maler Schreier GmbH, Ohorn
Exhibition design: Rimini Berlin/Jenny
Hasselbach, Marion Kliesch, Marx Werbung,
H. & M. Hildmann GbR, Pirna
Producing: KKS Architektur + Gestaltung,
Dresden/Hagen Engicht
Exhibition setup: Fißler & Kollegen GmbH,
Leipzig
Light design: Paul Göschel, Dresden
Video setup: Ralph Kunze, Produktionsbüro
Dresden/Dirk Preuß

Publication
Edited by Staatliche Kunstsammlungen
Dresden, Mathias Wagner, Hilke Wagner and
Kerstin Schankweiler, Kathleen Reinhardt

Staatliche Kunstsammlungen Dresden,
Albertinum
P.O. Box 120 551, 01006 Dresden
Tel.: +49 351 4914 2000
besucherservice@skd.museum
www.skd.museum

Conception: Kerstin Schankweiler,
Kathleen Reinhardt, Mathias Wagner
Editing: Martin Buhlig, Mathias Wagner,
Julia Hosp
Picture editing: Mathias Wagner, Pauline Hohn
Graphic design: Rimini Berlin/
Jenny Hasselbach, Franziska Morlok,
Fanny Liebhardt

Spector Books OHG, Harkortstraße 10,
04107 Leipzig
Project management: Jan Wenzel,
Marit Herrmann
Copy editing: Jan Caspers
Translation: Jan Caspers, Steven Lindberg,
Benjamin Schilling, Kate Vanovitch
Picture editing: Falk Messerschmidt, Leipzig
Printing: Gutenberg Beuys Feindruckerei
GmbH
Typography: Reader, Rosart
Paper: 100 g Munken Print White 15,
300 g Munken Print White 15

© 2024 Staatliche Kunstsammlungen
Dresden, Spector Books OHG, Leipzig,
authors, artists, photographers

1st Edition
www.spectorbooks.com
Book trade edition ISBN 978-3-95905-782-0
Museum edition ISBN 978-3-95905-784-4

The Deutsche Nationalbibliothek lists this
publication in the Deutsche National-
bibliografie; detailed bibliographic data are
available in the Internet at http://dnb.dnb.de.

Thanks to

Georges Adéagbo and Stephan Köhler,
Sven Johne, Hamlet Lavastida, Dana Lorenz,
Arlette Quỳnh-Anh Trần, Sonya Schönberger,
Wenke Seemann, Sung Tieu

Abed Abdi, Sven Barnick, Thomas Billhardt,
Jeanne Bindernagel, Herbert Boswank,
Carl Brunn, Giselher Blesse, Mona Bouguerba,
Guillermo J. Deisler, Anja Dworski, Hartwig
Ebersbach, Kathrin Barbara Franeck,
Dirk Gedlich, Lena Geuer, Denise Görlich,
Emmanuel Guiragossian, Carmelo Gonzáles
Gutiérrez, Peter Hartmann, Johannes Heisig,
Karsten Jahnke, Sandra Janßen, Nora
Kaschuba, Harald Kirschner, Annegret Klinker,
Gwendolin Kremer, Jule Lagoda, Ximena
León Pellegrin, André Lohmar, Michael
Mäder, Doreen Mende, Ivo Mohrmann,
Yvette Mutumba, Christina Nehrkorn-Stege,
Elke Neumann, Astrid Nielsen, Sigrid Noack,
César Olhagaray, Nora Riediger, Angela
Rietschel, Matthias Rietschel, Karla Sachse,
Kerstin Schankweiler, Uwe Schieferdecker,
Hans-Jörg Schirmbeck, Corinna Schröder,
Marina Schulz, Christian Saehrendt,
Uta Schnell, Olaf Simon, José Toirac, Tonel
(Antonio Eligio Fernández), Michael Touma,
Lutz Wohlrab, Meagane Zurfluh

As part of the program

Funded by

Funded by

Die Beauftragte der Bundesregierung
für Kultur und Medien

Exhibition support

Peter und Irene
Ludwig Stiftung

In cooperation with